CHRIST TO SALVATION

THE GOSPEL ACCORDING TO ZECHARIAH

PHILIP G. SAMAAN

Books by Philip G. Samaan

Christ's Way to Restoration
Christ's Way of Making Disciples
Christ Way to Spiritual Growth
Christ Way to Pray
Christ's Method Alone
Dare to Be a Daniel
Christ's Way of Affirmation
Abraham's Other Son
The Mideast Messiah

E-mail: pgs@southern.edu

CHRIST'S WAY TO SALVATION

THE GOSPEL ACCORDING TO ZECHARIAH

PHILIP G. SAMAAN

COLLEGE PRESS

Unless othe1wise noted, Bible texts are from the Revised
Standard Version of the Bible, copyrighted 1946, 1952 © 1971,
1973.

Texts credited to NIV are from the Holy Bible, New International Version. Copyright © 1973, 1978, International Bible
Society. Used by permission of Zondervan Bible Publishers.

Texts credited to NKN are from The New King James Version.
Copyright © 1979, 1980, 1982, Thomas Nelson, Inc., Publishers.

Verses credited to The Living Bible are copyrighted © 1971
by Tyndale House Publishers, Wheaton, Ill. Used by permission.

This book was
Edited by Richard W. Coffen
Designed by Megan Keller
Cover art by Greg Olsen
Type set: 9.9 Zapf Book Light

PRINTED IN U.S.A

94 93 92 91 90 89   10 9 8 7 6 5 4 3 2 1

224.98

ISBN 0-8280-0541-9

Printed by Review and Herald˙ Publishing Association
Reprinted by College Press Publishing LLC

Dedicated to

Jesus Christ,
our Savior and Lord,
and the fountain of our salvation
to the uttermost

Contents

Introduction

A story is told of an intriguing drawing of the American Declaration of Independence found in a museum of American history. To the casual and hurried onlooker, the drawing seems ambiguous and somewhat confusing because the artist arranged its different parts in such a subtle manner. However, on careful and repeated observation, a clear picture of the father of the American independence, George Washington, emerges from the seemingly unclear hues and arrangements of the various shapes and pieces.

Most visitors leave with just a fleeting impression of having seen a meaningless maze of scrambled lines, shades, and pieces. But to the few persisting and discerning observers, the face of George Washington leaps out from that important document, and looms great in their minds.

Likewise, the book of Zechariah may be compared to that drawing in the museum. Even though it is one of the most challenging and puzzling books in the Bible to understand, the brilliant face of the Messiah looks out from its pages on those who earnestly and patiently study it. Like a prism, Christ disperses beams of light from its different chapters to paint beautiful portraits of Himself.

He is God with us in a world of alienation and abandonment. He is our advocate and righteousness in a world of accusation and evil. He is our judge and vindicator in a world of chaos and oppression. He is our living branch that springs forth out of a dry ground. He is our only hope in a world of hopelessness. He is the compassionate good shepherd in a world full of evil shepherds who scatter the sheep. He is the suffering Messiah and the lamb slain from the foundation of the world.

Finally, Christ is the Saviour and Lord of the "Coming." He is love, and His love always seeks togetherness with us. That is His great desire: to come to us. Zechariah presents the three comings of Christ. His first coming to the people of Israel and to the entire world, bringing peace and salvation. Then His glorious second coming in the clouds of heaven to take the redeemed to the homes He prepared for them. After the millennium, Christ will come the third time as the judge of the whole world to establish His eternal kingdom. And sitting upon the great white throne, above the Holy City on the Mount of Olives, He will eradicate all evil, cleanse the earth with fire, and rule as King of kings and Lord of lords.

The book of Zechariah deserves much more attention on our part than we usually give it. There are a few very familiar verses that are quoted occasionally such as, "Not by might, nor by power, but by my spirit, saith the Lord of hosts" (Zech. 4:6, KJV). However, the major portions of the book are casually passed over. One of the main reasons that the book of Zechariah is somewhat unknown is because it is neglected and unopened.

Because the book of Zechariah is quite relevant to Seventh-day Adventist theology and mission, we need to study it earnestly. Considering its scope of 14 chapters, it is one of the most Messianic, eschatological, and apocalyptic books of the Old Testament. The book of Zechariah parallels the two books studied most thoroughly by Adventists, namely, the books of Daniel and Revelation. Even though it is considered a book among the Minor Prophets, it contains two chapters more than the book of Daniel. And it can be said that Zechariah and Daniel are the Old Testament equivalents of what Revelation is to the New Testament. One may imagine the prophet Zechariah standing between the prophet Daniel and the apostle John with extended arms, complementing and reinforcing their inspired messages.

The messages and prophecies of Zechariah came at a

crucial time in the history of God's people. Just returning from exile in Babylon, they were gripped with discouragement, spiritual lethargy, and uncertainty about the future. It was during such a prevailing mood that God called upon Zechariah to minister to His remnant people through His promises and restoration in the Messiah. So also does God call upon His remnant people of today to find revival and restoration in the timely messages of Zechariah emanating from the Messiah—His love, His life, and His return as King of kings and Lord of lords.

By Beholding Him

John Bunyan in his book *Pilgrim's Progress* describes the experience of the man with the muckrake. This man was so busy looking down and raking the dirt around him that he never stopped to look up and see an angel waiting to give him the crown of life. This muckraker was so preoccupied with the affairs of this life that he tragically missed out on eternal life. He never looked up and lived.

In this book, as we focus our attention on Christ, let us follow the example of the young prophet Zechariah. In the midst of his toil of ministering to his people, he was always aware of God's presence. He often stopped what he was doing to lift up his eyes and commune with Him. Zechariah's calling was very important indeed; however, the God who called him was even much more important.

How tragic it would be if we were to find ourselves in the same situation as Bunyan's muckraker. So caught up in this temporal life that we miss the everlasting life; and so preoccupied with the work of the Lord that we forget about the Lord of the work.

This certainly has been a universal spiritual hazard among God's people throughout the ages. It was the problem with the religious leaders during the time of Christ. But the rabbis did not have a monopoly on this problem. The disciples of Christ had their share of that problem, and we do too.

"In the estimation of the rabbis it was the sum of religion to be always in a bustle of activity. . . . The same dangers still exist. As activity increases and men become successful in doing any work for God, there is danger of trusting to human plans and methods. There is a tendency to pray less, and to have less faith. Like the disciples, we are in danger of losing sight of our dependence on God, and seeking to make a *savior* of our activity. We need to *look constantly* to Jesus, realizing that it is His power which does the work" (*The Desire of Ages*, p. 362; italics supplied).

With Zechariah, let us see visions of our Lord; let us see portraits of the Messiah; let us look up and live.

In studying the first six chapters of Zechariah, one cannot escape the fact that it was a habit, or a custom, with the prophet to look up and see a vision of God. Four times he refers to that in these chapters: 1:18; 2:1; 5:1; and 6:1. In the first two instances, Zechariah states, "And I lifted my eyes and saw . . ." Then in the remaining two verses, he describes his experience thus: "Again I lifted my eyes and saw . . ."

Zechariah's action of lifting up his eyes again and again to heaven has spiritual significance. He does not project himself to us as someone who faces his challenges alone, or broods over his problems without reaching beyond himself to God. Likewise, we all have our share of challenges and problems that we must face. However, long before we become burdened and obsessed with them, we must discipline ourselves over and over again to take them to Christ and see them from His perspective. Such challenges and problems will not disappear, but Christ will appear and face them with us. Before we become embroiled in trying to solve our problems down here, we must become absorbed in habitually lifting our eyes and looking up there.

Often we are aware of the natural realm, but rarely of the supernatural. Often we become so *attached* to the passing things of this world that we become *detached* from the realities of the world to come. Certainly the prayer of Elisha to God in behalf of his young assistant, "O Lord, I pray thee, *open his eyes* that he may see" (2 Kings 6:17), applies in full force to us living in this materialistic world. We must not naively hide our heads in the sand pretending all is well. Legions of Satan's forces surround us. But we must always be conscious of the fact that the invincible legions of the Lord of hosts also surround us.

John the Baptist experienced the supremacy of the supernatural over the natural because he looked up and saw a vision of God. "He looked upon the King in His beauty, and self was forgotten. He beheld the majesty of holiness, and felt himself to be inefficient and unworthy. He was ready to go forth as Heaven's messenger, *unawed by the human, because he had looked upon the Divine.* He could stand erect and fearless in the presence of earthly monarchs, because he had bowed low before the King of kings" (*ibid.*, p. 103; italics supplied).

We notice that Zechariah 5:1 and 6:1 introduce the word *again*, which signifies a pattern and a consistency in his communion with God. He did not lift up his eyes once, but repeatedly. One experience is not sufficient. We must look upon the Saviour again and again in order to replenish our spiritual reservoir and vitality. The Scriptures teach us about the necessity of such a continual spiritual experience. For example, they admonish us to pray without ceasing (1 Thess. 5:17), to die daily to self and to live for Christ (1 Cor. 15:31), to take up our cross daily and follow Christ (Luke 9:23), to delight ourselves with the law of God, to reflect on it day and night (Ps. 1:2), and to search the Word daily (Acts 17:11).

One day I was discussing with an acquaintance this biblical concept of continuous "looking up" and how absolutely essential it is for our spiritual survival and growth. He responded earnestly, saying, "I'm too busy, and I'm 'up to here' with my work. My life is very hectic, and I just don't have time to study and meditate." I asked gently if he had any time to eat. Slightly surprised, he responded, "Yes, of course, but that's different. If I don't eat, I won't be able to go on."

The last sentence that he uttered is obviously very true, and it ought to be as obvious also in the spiritual realm. We

need spiritual nourishment even more than physical nourishment because our eternal life depends on it. No job, no
activity, nothing whatsoever, is important enough to take us
away from taking the time to "look up" and commune with
our Lord. Simply put: look up and live. No time to look up,
no time to live.

Even the holy angels sense their need to commune with
God, and it is their greatest fulfillment and joy to be in His
presence. In her book *Steps to Christ*, Ellen White gives us
some very apt insight and counsel in this regard. "The
angels love to bow before God; they love to be near Him.
They regard communion with God as their highest joy; and
yet the children of earth, who need so much the help that
God only can give, seem satisfied to walk without the light of
His Spirit, the companionship of His presence" (p. 94).

Of course, Jesus affords our prime example in this
experience of continual and joyous communion with God.
In Mark 1:35 (NIV) it is recorded of Him that "very early in the
morning, while it was still dark, Jesus got up, left the house
and went off to a solitary place, where he prayed." He "went
off" to commune with His Father even though everyone was
looking for Him (verse 37).

Often we hear Christians comment on the many burdens and responsibilities they carry. They tell us that they
sincerely desire to spend quality time in their devotional life,
but, alas, they cannot because of lack of time or opportunity.
It is true, however, that we spend time, and sometimes
plenty of it, on what is important to us. Was not Jesus very
busy? Did He not have a lot of work? Obviously He did. "No
other life was ever so crowded with labor and responsibility
as was that of Jesus; yet how often He was found in prayer!
How *constant* was His communion with God! . . . In a life
wholly devoted to the good of others, the Saviour found it
necessary to withdraw from the thoroughfares of travel and
from the throng that followed Him day after day. He must
turn aside from a life of ceaseless activity and contact with
human needs, to seek retirement and *unbroken* communion

with His Father" (*The Desire of Ages*, pp. 362, 363; italics supplied).

Let us go back to Zechariah. Twice the word *turned* is used in describing his action of lifting up his eyes (Zech. 5:1; 6:1, KJV). In this context, the verb "turn" means to stop, change direction, interrupt what is being done, and contemplate doing something different. On a closer look at Zechariah 2:1; 5:1; and 6:1 we may glean the following progressive actions of the prophet. He (1) turned, (2) lifted up his eyes, (3) looked, and (4) beheld a vision.

As Zechariah went about his various busy activities of leading the returned exiles in rebuilding the ruins of the Temple and Jerusalem, he did not lose sight of God's presence. God was the first priority in his life. He was ready to interrupt his activities, no matter how important they were, lift up his eyes, and listen to God. He was never too busy to communicate with Him. That was his secret of spiritual victory, and it can be ours too.

Sometimes when things are going relatively well in our lives, we find it easy to pray and to "look up." But when the going gets tough, our faith gets shaky and discouragement sets in. It becomes very tempting to look horizontally rather than to look perpendicularly. In other words, during such trying times, it becomes easy to look at ourselves and others, and to complain and criticize instead of turning and lifting up our eyes to Christ. The tiny word *up* mentioned in Zechariah 5:1 and 6:1 is significant, and is often used in the Bible to show us our need to look beyond ourselves to God. In Isaiah 45:22 He invites us: "Look to Me, and be saved" (NKJV). And David declares, "To thee, O Lord, I lift up my soul" (Ps. 25:1). "We are to look away from self to Jesus" (*The Ministry of Healing*, p. 249).

As we reflect on the prophet Zechariah lifting up his eyes and seeing a vision of God, we are reminded of Proverbs 29:18, "Where there is no vision, the people perish." In the New International Version the word *revelation* is used instead of *vision*. Just as the man with the muckrake never stopped to lift up his eyes and so failed to receive the crown of life offered to him by the angel, so we also will not receive a vision—a revelation of God and His character, and an impartation of His love and life to us—unless we look up to Him. It awaits our reception. But we must ask for and appropriate what He longs to reveal to us. Without drawing on the Source, we separate ourselves from Him, and perish. Without looking up and seeing a vision of God, we miss out on the abundant life and will lose the crown of life. The good news is: it is there. Grasp it! Look up and live!

He Gives Repentance

Have you ever desired so much to go to Christ, but you could not get yourself to do it because you felt you were not good enough? At one point or another, we all have had such a needlessly frustrating experience. I was talking to a young man sometime ago about his sincere desire to submit himself to Jesus. Throughout our conversation, he kept reminding himself that he could not possibly go to Christ before he straightened out his life. He alluded to the fact that he had been trying to repent, and trying to have more faith, but to no avail.

It is sad that so many sincere people have so many misconceptions about God and the role He plays in our salvation. How much can a branch do to be alive and fruitful without the tree? Absolutely nothing. Jesus said, "I am the vine, you are the branches. He who abides in me, and I in him, he it is that bears much fruit, *for apart from me you can do nothing*" (John 15:5).

We often emphasize our return to God, and that is necessary. But do we also emphasize God's return to us? In this chapter we will explore this important subject, and see a loving portrait of Christ as one who has already taken the initiative in coming to us. He is the God who returns to us. He is the one who *gives* us faith and repentance and every impulse and every incentive to return to Him. How long have we delayed going to Christ in an effort to make ourselves better, while all along He has been yearning to embrace us with His love!

Our greatest qualification to go to Him is simply our need; therefore we all qualify. Do we need faith in order to return to Him? He gives us faith (1 Cor. 12:9; Eph. 2:8). Do we need true repentance? He also gives us repentance. Peter said of Christ: "The God of our fathers raised Jesus whom you killed by hanging him on a tree. God exalted him at his right hand as Leader and Savior, to *give repentance* to Israel and forgiveness of sins" (Acts 5:30, 31). Do we hesitate to go to Christ because of our heavy burdens? Well, He invites us: "Come unto me, all ye that labour and are heavy laden, and I will give you rest" (Matt. 11:28, KJV). "Do not listen to the enemy's suggestion to stay away from Christ until you have made yourself better; until you are good enough to come to God. If you wait until then, you will never come" (*Christ's Object Lessons*, pp. 205, 206).

Christ has come to us. He wants to give us faith, repentance, and forgiveness. He longs to take away our burdens of guilt and sin, and to give us His peace. Everything is ready, but we must go to Him. That all sounds so simple and inviting. Yes, but to go continually to Christ can be most challenging because this requires the giving of ourselves to Him.

As we focus on Zechariah 1:1-6, 12-17, we shall learn about God's return to His people and their return to Him in the context of reestablishing His covenant relationship with them. The following outline sheds some light on this issue:

God's Return
1. "I have returned to Jerusalem" (verse 16)
2. God's comforting words (verse 13)
3. God's great jealousy (verse 14)
4. God's great anger (verse 15)
5. God's great compassion (verse 16)

Israel's Return
1. God's earnest appeal, "Return to me" (verse 3)
2. God's exhortation, "Be not like your fathers" (verse 4)
3. Israel's spiritual returning (verse 6)

God's call to repentance through His prophet Zechariah is one of the strongest and most moving and spiritually intense calls of the entire Old Testament. The theme "Return to Me" took priority in Zechariah's ministry. Before He could restore Jerusalem and the Temple, God wanted to restore His covenant relationship with His people—He wanted their hearts first. He was willing to shower on them great blessings if they would just return to Him and walk in His ways.

Disillusionment had gripped the returning exiles. God intended that His invitation that His people return to Him infuse courage in their sagging morale and shore up their faith in Him. He had taken the initiative in restoring His covenant with them. He Himself had returned to them with mercy (verse 16).

God's plan of salvation—His covenant—has never changed. Moreover, His words and statutes are permanent and unchangeable. But His people do change, and their words and promises do not endure (verses 4-6). Still God loves His people and is jealous over them. He knows that a covenant relationship is reciprocal. He is returning to them, but the crucial question is Will *they* return to Him?

He is even willing to try different means to accomplish His covenant. He is willing to try again and again, but now for the last time He is earnestly pleading with His people through Zechariah to return to Him. Will they? He certainly wants them to reconstruct the Temple and Jerusalem, and He wants to usher in the Messianic age, but the *real* construction is not so much of brick and mortar, but is the *reconstruction of their hearts* after God.

God's thoughts about us and His ways of dealing with us are so wonderful that we can catch only a glimmer of them. "For as the heavens are higher than the earth, so are my ways higher than your ways and my thoughts than your thoughts" (Isa. 55:9). We cannot compare God to a human. When we are mistreated, we might hold a grudge or get a chip on the shoulder. We might act defensively, and usually we expect the guilty party to take the initiative toward us and make some amends. Still, the situation might never be restored completely.

God is not like that at all. His love is so pure, perfect, and overwhelming that even though He is the "injured party" in our relationship, and even though we leave Him for no reason, He is the one who seeks us out, pleading with us to return to Him, "no questions asked." So does He seek us out even when we do not seek Him? Yes. While we were His *enemies*—totally alienated from Him—"while we were yet sinners Christ died for us" (Rom. 5:8). Even when His people killed His messengers and prophets, Christ cried out, "How *often* I have *longed* to gather your children together, as a hen gathers her chicks under her wings, but you were *not willing*" (Matt. 23:37, NIV).

How do we explain this kind of behavior on God's part? It is a behavior that defies the most noble of human behavior and the greatest human imagination. The great Chinese philosopher Confucius spent his life attempting to develop a true state of human perfection. He was well known for his great nobility, love, and highest ethical standards. When asked what he thought of paying evil with kindness, he responded by saying that evil should not be treated with kindness but with justice.

Fortunately, our Lord responds differently: be kind and loving to those who are evil to you. And through Jeremiah He says, "I have loved you with an everlasting love; therefore I have continued my faithfulness to you" (Jer. 31:3). You see, short of undermining our freedom of choice, God is doing His best and utmost to woo us and to restore us to Him. But He needs us to respond to Him. And if a restored relationship does not result, it is absolutely not because of God's unwillingness but because of our unwillingness.

The theme of God's return to His people and their return to Him runs throughout the book of Zechariah. It is very important always to keep in mind that even though God's return to us is a proof of His love and acceptance, it will be of no avail unless we too return to Him. This theme of returning is emphasized and reinforced by the eight visions found in chapters 1:7 to 6:8.

In the first vision that Zechariah received (Zech. 1:8-17), we find an interesting dialogue between Christ, who is the Angel of the Lord (the man standing in the midst of the myrtle trees), and God the Father, who is the Lord of hosts. The response of the Father to His Son's question, "How long wilt thou have no mercy on Jerusalem?" (verse 12), has four pertinent elements in it pertaining to God's return. Let us look at these elements leading to the climax of the Lord of hosts' answer, "I have returned to Jerusalem with compassion" (verse 16).

God's Comfort. "And the Lord answered gracious and *comforting* words to the angel who talked with me" (verse 13). The returned exiles were discouraged and disheartened. What they needed most at this particular time were "gracious" words, words of comfort and affirmation. God discerned well their need, and in His love He met them where they were in order to lift up their spirits. Our God is a comforting God. He is the "God of all comfort" (2 Cor. 1:3) according to Paul. There is also tenderness in His comfort: "Comfort, comfort my people, says your God. Speak tenderly to Jerusalem" (Isa. 40:1, 2).

God's Great Jealousy. "Thus says the Lord of hosts: I am *exceedingly jealous* for Jerusalem and for Zion" (Zech. 1:14). Refer also to Zechariah 8:2. One talks about the problem or the sin of jealousy and people who are jealous. But what does it really mean for God to be jealous? The Hebrew word *qin'a* is translated "jealousy" in various versions of the Bible. However, the word can also mean zeal or fury. It may also refer to the color red in connection with someone becoming quite red in the face as a result of deep emotion. The Greek word for jealousy comes from the verb *zelein*, which means "to boil." One gets the impression from studying this word that it can be neutral in its meaning —not necessarily positive or negative in its connotation. It all depends on what it actually expresses.

When the intense emotion of jealousy is motivated by selfishness, it is negative and ultimately leads to hatred toward others. On the other hand, when this strong emotion is motivated by genuine concern, it is positive and results in love. In the context of Zechariah, it is a powerful expression of God's righteous indignation for the altruistic purpose of protecting, defending, chastising, and restoring His beloved people.

A beautiful picture of our Lord emerges from our study of this subject of divine jealousy. It reveals clearly the great intensity of His love toward His erring people. He is not at all passive or indifferent. His jealous and intense love is so great that He cannot sit still. He is moved to action. He rouses Himself from His holy dwellings (Zech. 2:13) to stand up for His wayward people. He is personally involved. We matter very much to Him; and He becomes angry and jealous over us. What a God! He cares, and He cares passionately for us. Don't we want to return to Him?

God's Great Anger. "And I am *very angry* with the nations that are at ease" (Zech. 1:15). God was greatly displeased or angry with the heathen nations. The Bible does not hesitate to describe God as angry or experiencing other strong emotions. It is the revulsion of His holy being to evil. It is said that God hates the sin but loves the sinner. That is very true. However, sin does not exist in a vacuum —it exists in people, and is practiced by people. God's anger reflects His great love and His concern that people leave sin alone.

Why was God very angry with the nations? Did He not use them to chastise His people by taking them captive? Yes, but those heathen nations, in their arrogance and pride, had overstepped all bounds in persecuting God's people. God was not *that* angry with Israel. God's anger with us shows that He cares. He would rather not chastise us, but if that is what it takes to propel us back to Him, He is willing. He cares enough to discipline us, but even in disciplining He takes care not to be too harsh. That is why He was sensitive when the nations went too far in punishing His people.

God's Great Compassion. "Therefore, thus says the Lord, I have returned to Jerusalem with *compassion*" (verse

16). What greater incentive can God give to draw His people to return to Him than to say that He has already returned to them? His goodness leads us to repentance (Rom. 2:4). His comforting words, His assurances, His initiatives, His divine jealousy and anger, and His compassion stir up in our hearts the longing to go back to Him. Jesus said, "And I, when I am lifted up from the earth, will draw all men to myself" (John 12:32). God has indeed returned to us in the person of the crucified Christ. He is drawing us to Himself. Shall we not return to Him?

Zechariah 1:3 is the key text in which God appeals to His people to return to Him. Let us look at it further in the following outline:

"Thus says the Lord of hosts"
"Return to me"
"Says the Lord of hosts"
"And I will return to you"
"Says the Lord of hosts"

The text above shows how God's appeal for us to return is paralleled with His promise to return. It is prefaced, punctuated, and concluded with the phrase "says the Lord of hosts." This clearly shows how serious and earnest God is in His appeal. In just one verse He gives His solemn word by invoking His special title "Lord of hosts" three times.

In this earnest appeal, God wants to make a complete break with the past and begin afresh with the returned and chastised exiles. His invitation to return to Him included not only mention of the benefits that would result, but also words of exhortation and warning. This was a serious matter, because a genuine return to God should include giving up false security and presumption.

In the Bible the word *return* to God is close in meaning to the word *repent*. It is usually addressed to a person who has turned his back on God, gradually going further and further away from Him. To "return" means to stop, to cease turning one's back on God, and to start walking in the opposite direction—toward God. This is the only way to benefit from God's returning and to appropriate His promises. God has made Himself available for the renewal of the covenant relationship, but we have to make ourselves available too.

The literal return of the Jews from Babylon had taken place. But only a minority heeded God's invitation to return to Jerusalem. The majority stayed in the comforts of Babylon. Ellen White, quoting Zechariah 2:6-9, explains that God "inspired Zechariah to plead with the exiles to return. . . . The large number, however, of those who failed to respond to the decree of Cyrus, remained unimpressible to later influences; and even when Zechariah warned them to flee from Babylon without further delay, they did not heed the invitation" (*Prophets and Kings*, pp. 599, 600).

Now God calls the remnant who came out of Babylon and settled in Jerusalem to a *spiritual return* to Him. The call involved much more than the building of the Temple. It involved the rebuilding of a temple in their hearts for God to dwell in. We must build on Christ first before we try to build other things. The apostle Paul writes, "For no other foundation can any one lay than that which is laid, which is Jesus Christ" (1 Cor. 3:11). And David declares, "Unless the Lord builds the house, those who build it labor in vain" (Ps. 127:1).

Is it possible for an individual, in a certain sense, to come out of Babylon but still be in Babylon? Can we perhaps be members of the remnant church but in our hearts still be in Babylon? Can there possibly be some in Babylon whose hearts are after God? There must not only be a physical coming out, but more important, a coming out and staying out of the mind and heart. "Not withstanding the spiritual darkness and alienation from God that exist in the churches which constitute Babylon, the great body of Christ's true followers are still to be found in their communion" (*The Great Controversy*, p. 390).

God also appeals to His people to learn valuable lessons from their past so that they will not be condemned to repeat it. He exhorts them, "Be not like your fathers" (Zech. 1:4). He entreats them to learn from the mistakes of their fathers, make a radical break with the past, and have a fresh start by trusting Him and His word. In Zechariah 1:5, 6, He contrasts the passing away of the fathers and the prophets with the endurance of God's words and statutes. His words overtook their fathers. The fathers heard the words of God, and they perished. The prophets preached the words of God, and they passed away. But the words of God overtook all and still remain. The words of God, in the long run, catch up with every one, no matter who. They tried to ignore and run away from them, but finally His words outlasted them.

God in effect is saying that there is no way His people can make it without Him, try as they may. If we are to succeed, we must be connected to God and His Word. People die, circumstances change, events pass away, but God and His Word march on forever. No matter what we do, God's words will confront and overtake us either to confirm or to condemn us.

God has returned to us. Let us without any delay return to Him and remain with Him.

God
With Us

One of the most important and meaningful things about having true friends is the joy of *being with them*. We all have experienced the exhilarating feeling of anticipating the arrival of good friends whom we had not seen for some time. Why? Because we know we are going to be with them, sharing and doing things together that we mutually enjoy. In such genuine relationships, we feel acceptance, affection, and affirmation. We feel at ease with such friends, and we enjoy their company.

When the New Testament writers wanted to express God's great love, they found the neutral Greek word *agape* and filled it with all of what God is like. That is why John, the disciple whom Jesus loved, was inspired to write one of the most profound truths in the entire Bible: "God is love" (1 John 4:8). God is agape love personified, and this love has different characteristics. One of these important characteristics of God's love is that it is never alone and that it always seeks *togetherness*.

If we love someone, we are drawn to be with that person. On the other hand, if we cannot stand somebody, we find ourselves dreading times of togetherness and quite possibly trying to avoid such a person. The good news about God is that He does not avoid us. Instead, He is drawn to us no matter who we are. He seeks to be with us and cherishes our company.

In fact, we find this theme dominant in the Scriptures. God greatly desires to be with us. Such an emphasis should prove to us beyond a shadow of a doubt that He indeed loves us. An abundance of examples reveals this fact from the Old Testament and from the New. During their sojourn in the wilderness God tells the children of Israel through Moses, "And let them make me a sanctuary, that I may *dwell in their midst*" (Ex. 25:8). Then about 15 centuries later, "the Word became flesh and made his *dwelling among us*" (John 1:14, NIV). The same Jesus the Word who dwelt in their midst in the wilderness is the same person who became a man, making His residence among them.

But He is not satisfied to dwell with His people only in this temporal world. He desires to dwell with them for eternity in His glorious kingdom. As Jesus neared His crucifixion, He solemnly promised His disciples: "I am going there to prepare a place for you. And if I go and prepare a place for you, I will come back and take you *to be with me* that you also may be where I am" (John 14:2, 3, NIV).

In Bible times names had special significance. A name represented one's character and reputation. Christ was also given a special name, Immanuel, which means "God with us." That name flashes a clear message across Planet Earth that God intends and desires to be with His people. That name embodies the whole meaning of salvation in one word. "Behold, a virgin shall be with child, and shall bring forth a son, and they shall call his name Emmanuel, which being interpreted is, God with us" (Matt. 1:23, KJV; see also Isa. 7:14).

Three visions, which clearly show that God is present in the midst of His people, reinforce God's appeal to His people through Zechariah to return to Him, for He has returned to them. The first vision: the man among the myrtle trees (Zech. 1:7-17). The second vision: the four horns and four artisans (verses 18-21). The third vision: the man with the measuring line (Zech. 2:1-13).

There is more to these visions than the minute details and what is apparent on the surface. God is aroused to action in behalf of His discouraged people. Yes, He wants to reestablish His people in their land, but more important, He

Himself wants to be reestablished in their hearts. He wants to help them rebuild the Temple, but even more crucial than that, He desires to help them rebuild His temple in their hearts so that He might dwell in them. He is ready to assist them in restoring the walls around Jerusalem, but more urgent than that, He Himself wants to be their wall of defense and protection.

The Man Among the Myrtle Trees. In this first vision, Zechariah looks up and sees a man riding a red horse among the myrtle trees. This same man is referred to as "the angel of the Lord" in the vision. Zechariah 1:11 makes it clear that they are the same person. "And they answered the angel of the Lord that stood among the myrtle trees, and said, We have walked to and fro through the earth, and, behold, all the earth sitteth still, and is at rest" (KJV). This same reference to "the angel of the Lord" appears again in the fourth vision, and is mentioned twice by that exact name in 3:1, 6 in the heavenly court scene as the advocate of Joshua.

This "angel of the Lord" is distinguished from the interpreting angel, who accompanies the prophet throughout the visions and whom Zechariah refers to consistently with the exact same words as "the angel who talked with me" (Zech. 1:9, 13). Also this interpreting angel is described with these same words in other verses such as Zechariah 1:19; 2:3; 4:1, 4, 5; 5:5; and 6:4. The identities of these two different angels are well established and clearly distinguishable.

Jesus Christ, the first person of the Godhead, is that angel of the Lord. Biblical evidence clearly shows this fact. (See Ex. 3:2, 4; Zech. 3:1, 2; cf. Gen. 32:24; Joshua 5:13-15.) He is the one who appeared to Moses, Jacob, and Joshua; and now in our study He appears to Zechariah. He is the Christ who asks the "Lord of hosts," who is God the Father, this passionate question of how long will it take till He restores His people (Zech. 1:12).

Christ's inquiry of His Father reveals His great love and concern as the mediator in behalf of the people. Also it is important to note that the Father's response shows no less love and compassion than the Son's. God the Father loves us as much as His Son. It is heartening to realize that They do converse with Each Other about us, that we do matter to Them, and that They do take our problems seriously. What great Friends to have! They not only care greatly about our difficulties, but They are able and willing to do something about them. What other friends in this world are able or willing to do that?

Zechariah 1:8, 10 tells us that Christ was standing *among* the myrtle trees. What do these myrtle trees possibly signify? Quite likely these trees symbolize the returned exiles and God's love and grace that He was bestowing upon them. This likelihood is enhanced by the following considerations. Let us have a careful look at them:

1. Myrtle trees were a familiar sight in Israel and Judah. They were common in Palestine and plentiful around Jerusalem (Neh. 8:15; Isa. 41:19). This tree is also "quite likely the evergreen *Myrtus communis*, which bears snow-white flowers bordered with purple and an aromatic fruit from which perfumes are made. . . . Myrtle branches were used to build booths for the Feast of Tabernacles in postexilic Jerusalem (Neh. 8:15)" (*SDA Bible Dictionary*, p. 770).

2. Zechariah was shown this "angel of the Lord," Christ, standing among these myrtle trees. This fact is certainly consistent with the whole thrust of this first vision and also of the third one that God wants to dwell in the midst of His people. Hence, Christ among the myrtle trees is the equivalent of Christ among His people.

3. The grand theme of God returning to His people and being in their midst is the very central theme of the entire book of Zechariah and the subject of restoration. So Christ's standing among the myrtle trees is consistent with this central theme.

4. Myrtle branches were used in the building of the booths for the Feast of Tabernacles. This feast was celebrated in the fall at the end of the dry season in great anticipation of God manifesting Himself among them via the

torrents of rain. Jesus attended a Feast of Tabernacles celebrated in Jerusalem. It is significant that on the last day of this feast He offered Himself as the water of life and the promise of the Spirit as the ultimate manifestation of God's presence and blessings among His people.

"On the last day of the feast, the great day, Jesus stood up and proclaimed, 'If any one thirst, let him come to me and drink. He who believes in me, as the scripture has said "Out of his heart shall flow rivers of living water" ' " (John 7:37, 38).

5. Zechariah is a very Messianic book, and Christ is the very heart and center of it. With all His earnest appeals to His demoralized people, and His longing to be with them and restore them, it would seem natural and consistent that He would want to be among them like He was seen among the myrtle trees.

What does this tell us about Christ? He is not someone who absents Himself, but rather He stands up for His discouraged people and comes to be with them in sympathy and solidarity. And as a result of His presence among them, many blessings are bestowed. Zechariah 1:13-17 mentions some of these great blessings. He gives them His comfort, love, defense, compassion, prosperity, and restoration.

It is interesting to observe that the names of Jerusalem, Judah, and Zion are mentioned several times in Zechariah 1. This feature is also evident throughout the book. "Jerusalem" is mentioned by name 41 times, and "Judah" is mentioned 21 times. It is true that we tend to think of and mention names of individuals near and dear to us. The Lord, here in this passage and in all Zechariah, is apparently so absorbed with love for His people that He mentions their names very frequently.

The Four Horns and the Four Artisans. This short vision comprises only four verses: two questions and two answers. We find the young prophet Zechariah to be always keen and alert, and he barely hears the response to his first question before he plunges into his second question. The first question and answer relate to the four horns, and the second question and answer relate to the four artisans. This vision is a dialogue between Zechariah and the angel who talked with him.

The word *horn* occurs frequently in the Scriptures. In prophecy it represents political power, kings, or kingdoms (as in Dan. 7:8, 20, 21; Rev. 17:12, 16). This is the meaning that applies to the four horns in the context of this vision. "Horn" may also mean strength, boldness, and arrogance—just as an animal uses its horns to boast of its strength and employs them either defensively or offensively. (See Ps. 75:4, 5; 132:17.)

"What are these?" (Zech. 1:18) Zechariah asks the inter-preting angel of the four horns. The angel's response clearly identifies these horns as the powers that had "scattered Judah, Israel, and Jerusalem" (verse 19). The number four probably corresponds to the four compass points—north, east, south, and west—hence the universal application to the entire heathen world.

Interestingly, Zechariah's question referring to the four horns is concerned with their *identity:* "What are these?" However, in his second question, referring to the four artisans, he is concerned about *function*: "What are these coming to do?" (verse 21). This indicates that the artisans are here to act and that the horns are the recipients of such action (verse 21).

The word *carpenters* found in the King James Version, and the word *smiths* mentioned in the Revised Standard Version come from the Hebrew word *charashim*, which means "artisans"—workers in metal, wood, and stone. How-ever, the word used in the New International Version, *craftsmen*, is closer to the original meaning of the word. These four artisans—or craftsmen—represent God's agen-cies that would stand up for His people and against the four horns "which scattered Judah, Israel, and Jerusalem" in order "to cast" them down (verses 19, 21).

Biblical scholars have made many conjectures as to the identity of the four horns and the four artisans. For example, some have interpreted the four horns to mean the four hostile empires that persecuted and scattered Israel—Babylon, Medo-Persia, Greece, and Rome. It suffices to state that these heathen powers would have their turn at being terrified and cast down by the artisans, experts in works of wood, stone, and metal, who represented "the agencies used by the Lord in restoring His people and the house of His worship" (*Prophets and Kings*, p. 581).

What does the vision of the four horns and the four artisans teach us about how the Lord works in the affairs of His people and the world? God is intimately acquainted with the affairs of humanity. He is the one who really knows everything—past, present, and future. With all His knowledge, He uses opportunities and circumstances in history to help His people. That is why He wants to walk among them and dwell in their midst, for He wants to act in their behalf.

We can glean other spiritual lessons from this vision. God is a realist. He does not just offer solutions to problems, but He also exposes such problems for what they are. He shows Zechariah not only the artisans but also the horns. He does not want us to hide our heads in the sand, pretending all is well. There are indeed horns out there surrounding us from all directions, but, thank God, we are also surrounded by His craftsmen, who are able and ready to cast down these menacing horns. There is the danger, however, that we might see only the first part of Zechariah's vision, the horns, and as a result become so obsessed with them and frightened by them that we do not see the second part of the vision, God's solution—His able craftsmen.

The four craftsmen also tell us that when the Lord dwells in our midst, everything is possible. No matter how mighty the horns of our problems may be, or how many of them we might face, God's craftsmen are more than a match to every one of them. For the four horns, there are the four craftsmen. And for every horn, God has just the right craftsman to deal with it.

Finally, in the Bible, "craftsmen" or "artisans" refer to specialists in working with wood—carpenters; specialists in working with stone—masons; and specialists in working with metal—smiths. Symbolically speaking, we might be facing "wooden" horns—not very hard, or "stony" horns—hard, or "metallic" horns—very hard. The good news is that God does have His divine specialists who know how to handle all kinds of horns. The carpenters, the masons, and the smiths know how to cut, break, and melt whatever horns dare to lift themselves up against us.

The Man With the Measuring Line. This third vision, recorded in Zechariah 2:1-13, also shows the future greatness of Israel as a nation resulting from God's presence with them. But we know that such glorious prospects were not fulfilled to literal Israel, not because God failed, but because Israel failed. It is important to understand that ultimately God's plan will not change, and it will succeed regardless of human failure of any group or nation. The ways of accomplishing such a plan may change on account of human changeability and God's respect for man's freedom of choice.

In *Prophets and Kings*, we learn of how God modified the manner of accomplishing His eternal plan: "That which God purposed to do for the world through Israel, the chosen nation, He will finally accomplish through His church on earth today" (p. 713). No matter how much God wants to remain with His people, it is of no avail unless they also want Him to remain with them. He will not force Himself on them. Even when He respects their choice by allowing them to leave Him, He cries out for them: "How can I give you up, O Ephraim! How can I hand you over, O Israel!" (Hosea 11:8).

The apostle Paul clarifies this transition from literal Israel to spiritual Israel in Romans 9-11. He affirms that God will keep His promises, which will be realized through spiritual Israel or the Christian church. In Romans 9:30, 31 he states specifically that spiritual Israel has taken the place of literal Israel, and that everyone who accepts Christ and experiences His abiding presence will become a part of God's spiritual Israel.

The young man with the measuring line was stopped from completing his work of measuring Jerusalem. Why did the angel stop him? In studying Zechariah 2:4, 5, we discover two reasons why Jerusalem would not have walls around it:

1. The vastness and richness of God's blessings. Because of the multitudes of people and cattle coming into it from other nations, there will be no way to contain such a vast multitude with walls. The spread of Jerusalem's vastness, greatness, and influence will go far beyond any limiting walls. (See Zech. 2:4.)

2. The Lord's presence in their midst. Outwardly, God "will be unto her a wall of fire round about" referring to His defense and protection against her enemies. Inwardly, God "will be the glory in the midst of her," referring to His divine presence. (See Zech. 2:5, KJV.)

The theme of God's presence in the midst and around His people (represented by glory, fire, and light) is a very important one in the Bible. Christ Himself is the pillar of cloud and the pillar of fire (Ex. 13:21, 22; Neh. 9:12). The Lamb is the light and glory of Jerusalem (Rev. 21:23, 24). God gave this vision to assure His people that He was with them. They were not sure He was. Because they looked at the unfinished Temple, symbolizing God's presence, and at the ruined city walls for security and protection, they wondered if God had left them and had forgotten them. They also had the painful inward feeling that the Temple and the city, even if completed, would not recover their former glory and grandeur.

They were looking for assurance in buildings and walls, in past glory. And here is where God met them, at their point of need. In Zechariah 1 He appealed to them to trust His words. Now in chapter 2, He appeals to them to trust in His mighty and glorious presence with and around them. They must place their trust not so much in walls and buildings but in Him, for He was pledging Himself to them.

When the Romans entered Jerusalem in A.D. 70, they cast a big fiery torch into the Temple and ransacked Jerusalem. What happened to God's promise of inward glory and light and outward protection and security? That wall of fire and that light and glory were not quenched and taken away by God's choice, but by the Jews, who did not remain faithful to their part of the covenant. Tragically, they had forgotten their God, and their sins had driven Him away from them. Consequently they were left to reap the natural results of their rebellion. (See Hosea 8:14; Amos 2:5; Matt. 23:37, 38.)

"Zechariah's messages, setting forth Jerusalem's glorious future, were conditional (Zech. 6:15). Because of the failure of the Jews, when they returned from captivity, to meet the spiritual conditions upon which their prosperity was based, the prophecies were not fulfilled in their original intent. However, certain features will be fulfilled in the Christian church" (The SDA Bible Commentary, vol. 4, p. 1085).

The promises made to the Jews were transferred to the church and its members, who were once in darkness but who now had become light in the Lord (Eph. 5:8). His light and glory shines through them who are "the light of the world" (Matt. 5:14-16) and who reflect His light and glory. The Christian church, God's faithful remnant, was protected and preserved throughout the centuries by God's "wall of fire"—His presence in it. Walls could not contain the expansion of that church. Through the power, light, and presence of God, it expanded to all the then-known world, and it continues to expand in the world today as it evangelizes the world, preparing it to enter "the holy city, new Jerusalem, coming down out of heaven from God" (Rev. 21:2). That New Jerusalem will have the glory of God (verse 11)—and "the glory of God is its light, and its lamp is the Lamb" (verse 23).

What limiting "measuring lines" do we use in our lives and in our church? What are the "walls" of security in our lives? In what do we put our trust today? We may have our goals and plans, our own measuring line, but God too has His goals and plans for us and our churches. Are we sometimes so absorbed in our measurings that we lose sight of what God is trying to do in us and through us?

There are always the statisticians and goal-setters who want to count and measure everything they can get their hands on. No doubt this is needed and useful. However, we must be careful not to set limits and not to define rigidly God's work and plans. Let us keep in mind that He is thinking of fire, light, and glory! How can we measure that! Or can we measure and define the limits of a loving and kind act? What about God's love? It is so great and vast, so potent and limitless, that no walls can contain it in the human heart, in the church, or in the world at large.

As we come to the conclusion of this chapter, we shall look at some important points found in Zechariah 2:10-13, 8, which relate to God's promise of dwelling in Zion, inheriting Judah, and choosing Jerusalem so that whoever touches them touches the apple of His eye. Also in verses 10, 11 twice appears the declaration of the Lord, "I will dwell in the midst of you," and as a result of that "many nations shall join themselves to the Lord" (verse 11).

"In view of the glorious prospect, Zion is called upon to rejoice. If the people had heeded the messages of its prophets, the city would have 'stood forth in the pride of prosperity, the queen of kingdoms' (*The Desire of Ages*, p. 577). God would have dwelt in the midst of her and Jerusalem would have become the world's diadem of glory. With the failure of Israel and the accomplishment of God's purposes in the spiritual seed, the Christian church. . . , the ground of rejoicing is now the New Jerusalem 'coming down from God out of heaven' " (*The SDA Bible Commentary*, vol. 4, p. 1091).

Let us consider Zechariah 2:12 in light of the New Testament and the Christian church:

1. The Lord *inheriting* Judah. The Christians through Christ become *"heirs* of God, and *joint-heirs* with Christ" (Rom. 8:17, KJV). "And if you are Christ's, then you are *Abraham's offspring, heirs* according to promise" (Gal. 3:29).

2. The Lord *choosing* Jerusalem. Also Christians through Christ are *chosen* by Christ (John 15:16). "But you are a *chosen* race" (1 Peter 2:9).

The Apple of His Eye. The Hebrew word for "apple" in Zechariah 2:8 is *babah*, which can mean "the eyeball." The eyeball is extremely sensitive, even to small irritations and dust particles. Obviously, one is extremely sensitive to someone poking a finger in his eye. Two references in the Bible speak of "the apple of his eye," Zechariah 2:8 and Deuteronomy 32:10.

The point cannot be missed: God is very loving and sensitive to us. The verse tells us this in a very personal and intimate way. We have a God who is very protective of us. We all know how sensitive and precious our eyes are to us, and how protective we are of them, especially if someone tries to poke something into them. *The Living Bible* uses an interesting way to paraphrase Zechariah 2:8: "He who harms you sticks his finger in Jehovah's eye!" And He says this about His unfaithful people!

Yes, to touch us is to poke God in the eye! He is God with us. He identifies intimately with us. He is in our midst. We are in His heart. We are the apple of His eye.

Christ
Our Advocate

Who would not want to retain a good defense attorney if accused of a serious crime? We all would for sure. We also would want a reputable judge to preside over the case. Why? Because there would also be in the same courtroom a tough prosecuting attorney who would push his case against us to the limit. He would throw at us everything in the book, and maybe more.

The above is a hypothetical situation. However, the case of every person in the heavenly court is not at all hypothetical. We had better have a very good advocate and judge, because there is also in the same heavenly courtroom a very tough prosecutor, Satan our adversary, "the accuser of our brethren, . . . who accuses them day and night before our God" (Rev. 12:10). His expertise is in accusation, and he has developed this specialty into a fine art that he plies without ceasing—and dares to do it in the heavenly courtroom even in the presence of God Himself. The facts of the case are that we are indeed guilty, and prosecutor Satan is demanding the maximum sentence, the death penalty.

But, thank God, it does not end there. We do have a defense Attorney who is more than a match for Satan. He also is an expert—an expert at defending us. Our defense is the total commitment of our mighty Petitioner, who "is able for all time to save those who draw near to God through him, since he always lives to make intercession for them" (Heb. 7:25).

What a vast difference exists between our accuser and

our Advocate! Satan lives to accuse and destroy, but Christ lives to defend and save to the uttermost in mercy and righteousness.

Zechariah portrays Christ our Advocate and is our focus in this chapter. Consider the following overview of Zechariah's fourth vision in chapter three before we proceed further in this very important study:

The Heavenly Court
1. The accused (verses 1, 3)
2. The accuser (verse 1)
3. The Advocate (verses 1, 2)

The Defense
1. Satan rebuked (verse 2)
2. A brand plucked out of the fire (verse 2)

Vindication and Restoration
1. Covering: justification (verses 4, 5)
2. Walking (here): sanctification (verse 7)
3. Walking (there): glorification (verse 7)

First, we need to review the historical context of this very important vision. The recently returned exiles from Babylon were like "a brand plucked from the fire" (verse 2). They were almost consumed in the fires of hardship, despair, and persecution. In fact, they would have been completely destroyed had not their merciful God intervened just in time. Joshua, in this vision, represents the people, standing in their place as their high priest. He is the central *human* figure in this vision, on whom the righteousness of Christ was so generously bestowed. "The Angel of the Lord," Christ the Advocate, the second person in the Godhead, is the central *divine* figure.

Satan the accuser was taking full advantage of the vulnerable position the people found themselves in. Since they were down, he thought that was an ideal time to unleash all his forces against them so he could finish them off for good. Also Satan was quite alarmed to see some progress in the building of the Temple, and he wanted to snuff out this last ray of hope. He was "determined to put forth still further effort to weaken and discourage God's people by holding before them their imperfections of character" (*Prophets and Kings*, p. 582).

But God, who does not slumber or sleep, was also there, and "through an impressive illustration of the work of Satan and the work of Christ, He showed the power of their Mediator to vanquish the accuser of His people" (*ibid.*, p. 583).

This specific message in Zechariah's fourth vision does have a relevant, peculiar, and urgent application for God's remnant people now and in the near future. We who live in the last days of earth's history just before the close of probation *must* study, experience, and share this vitally important message from God.

"I entreat of you . . . read the third and fourth chapters of Zechariah. If these chapters are understood, if they are received, a work will be done for those who are hungering and thirsting for righteousness, a work that means to the church: 'Go forward and upward' " (*Testimonies*, vol. 6, p. 296). "Zechariah's vision of Joshua and the Angel applies with peculiar force to the experience of God's people in the closing scenes of the great day of atonement" (*Prophets and Kings*, p. 587).

The Heavenly Court Scene. We are indeed fortunate to see the curtain that separates the seen and the unseen world rolled back and to gain a glimpse of the great controversy going on between good and evil. (Compare Zechariah 3:1-7 with the heavenly court scene in Job 1:6-12.) Here Zechariah sees a heavenly court scene complete with the defendant, the prosecutor, the defense attorney, the witnessing angels, and the judge.

God the Father is there as the presiding judge. He is "the Lord" mentioned three times in Zechariah 3:2 who rebukes Satan. He is the same "Lord" and "Lord of hosts" mentioned earlier in Zechariah 1:10, 12, 13, 14, 16, and 17. He is to be distinguished from "the angel of the Lord," or "the angel" whom Joshua "was standing before" (Zech. 3:1, 3). The Angel is Christ the Advocate, the second person in the Godhead, who ordered the filthy garments to be removed from Joshua (verse 4).

We must remember, however, that the Father and the Son cooperate together in our defense. The Bible teaches that God the Father is indeed the judge but that He delegated this responsibility to His Son. Jesus Himself said, "The Father judges no one, but has given all judgment to the Son" (John 5:22). Paul calls Jesus "the righteous judge" (2 Tim. 4:8). Therefore Christ not only is our able advocate, but He is also our righteous judge and compassionate high priest.

The Accused. It is helpful to learn more about Joshua the high priest and to compare him to Christ our heavenly high priest. Joshua the son of Jehozadak was the first high priest after the return from Babylon (Haggai 1:1, 12, 14; Ezra 2:2; Neh. 7:7). His father had been the last high priest, whom Nebuchadnezzar had taken captive to Babylon, and probably his son Joshua had been born there in exile (1 Chron. 6:15). Joshua's grandfather, Seraiah, who was also a high priest, had been tragically executed at Riblah by the Babylonian king (2 Kings 25:18-21).

In the Hebrew and Greek languages the names *Joshua* and *Jesus* are identical. Joshua is the Hebrew form, and Jesus is the Greek form. So both names mean "Yahweh is the Saviour." In Matthew 1:21 we read, "Thou shalt call his name Jesus: for he shall save his people from their sins" (KJV). How relevant for the high priest to be called Joshua! The great problem of Israel was the mountain of sins that separated them from God. In this fourth vision Joshua is in a certain sense a type of Christ our faithful high priest. Joshua represents his sinful people, and becomes their substitute before the tribunal of heaven. He is a type of the Servant Branch who "will remove the guilt of this land in a single day" (Zech. 3:8, 9; see also Zech. 6:11-13).

Joshua "was clothed with filthy garments" (Zech. 3:3, KJV). These "filthy garments" parallel Isaiah's "filthy rags"— they represent our true condition, and even our best condition, or all of our human righteousness. For Isaiah declares, "But we are all like an unclean thing, and all our righteousnesses are like filthy rags" (Isa. 64:6, NKJV). Oh how desperately we all need the perfect righteousness of Christ our advocate and high priest!

We cannot help noticing that Joshua said absolutely nothing to defend himself. He did not utter one single word of excuse. He simply stood there, recognizing his guilt and his people's guilt and submitting himself to God's mercy. And that is exactly the kind of attitude we need to have.

We may glean five steps for silencing the accuser and receiving our Redeemer's righteousness from the study of this pertinent statement found in *Prophets and Kings*: "The high priest cannot defend himself or his people from Satan's accusations. He does not claim that Israel is free from fault. In filthy garments, symbolizing the sins of the people, which he bears as their representative, he stands before the Angel, confessing their guilt, yet pointing to their repentance and humiliation, and relying upon the mercy of a sin-pardoning Redeemer. In faith he claims the promises of God" (pp. 583, 584).

1. Joshua does not defend or excuse his sin.
2. He confesses his people's guilt.
3. He points to their repentance and humiliation.
4. He relies on the Redeemer's mercy.
5. In faith he claims God's promises.

Ellen White has given us another great spiritual formula: look away from self and Satan, and *look up* to our Advocate and Redeemer. "When Satan comes to tell you that you are a great sinner, *look up* to your Redeemer and talk of His merits. . . . Acknowledge your sin, but tell the enemy that 'Christ Jesus came into the world to save sinners,' and that you may be saved by His matchless love" (*Steps to Christ*, pp. 35, 36; italics supplied).

That is the greatest work we may do—going to Christ and remaining with Christ. Our part is not to defend ourselves. That is the work of our Defender; let us let Him do His work! He offers in Himself our greatest defense. Our part is to look up to Him. Look at what happens when we try to defend ourselves or excuse our faults. "If those who hide and excuse their faults could see how Satan *exults* over them, how he *taunts* Christ and holy angels with their course, they would make *haste* to confess their sins and to put them away" (*The Great Controversy*, p. 489; italics supplied).

The Accuser. Even though Satan is there in the heavenly court "to accuse" Joshua (Zech. 3:1), we do not learn exactly what he said. Of course, he does not need to say too much there, because he has been accusing Joshua and his people before God full time, "day and night" (Rev. 12:10). He has his case thoroughly prepared against them. He is also fully acquainted with each one of our cases. He has done all the research, and he is always ready to prosecute and to push his case against us to the fullest.

The apostle Peter sheds additional light on the identity and function of Satan the accuser. He considers him to be a fierce and wily person and warns us to watch out for him. He admonishes us to "be sober, be watchful. Your adversary the devil prowls around like a roaring lion, seeking some one to devour" (1 Peter 5:8). The Hebrew word for Satan is the same as in English, *haśśatan*, which literally means "the adversary" or "the accuser." The word translated "resist" in the King James Version in Zechariah 3:1 also comes from the Hebrew verb *śatan*, meaning literally "to accuse."

Here in this vision we see Satan as a real person going about his business. He is not the figment of someone's imagination, a mere idea, or just an evil force. He clearly comes across as a specific individual who accuses Joshua and confronts his Advocate, Christ. He also seems to act as an official in the heavenly court, for he stands at the right hand of Joshua the accused—the normal position of a prosecuting attorney.

Does Christ tolerate His archenemy to come into His holy presence? Christ has absolutely nothing to fear of Satan. He vanquished him at the cross, and He holds his very life in His hand. He does not try to hide Satan in some corner, silencing him from making accusations. He wants the truth to be known and Satan to be revealed for who he truly is. If Satan thinks he has a case to present, then let him present it, and the truth will ultimately win out.

But what motivates Satan to level his accusations against God's people so relentlessly? He contests Christ's right to forgive and rescue them, because he claims that they are undeserving and that they are his own possession. He becomes very angry and determined whenever a poor soul seeks rescue in Christ. "*Never* is one received into the family of God without exciting the *determined* resistance of the enemy" (*Prophets and Kings*, p. 585; italics supplied). He also has an intense hatred of Christ. In attacking God's people, Satan wants to get back at our Saviour and His plan of salvation. "His accusations arise from his enmity to Christ. . . . All the hatred and malignity of the archrebel is stirred as he beholds the evidences of Christ's supremacy; and with fiendish power and cunning he works to wrest from Him the children of men who have accepted salvation" (*ibid.*, p. 586).

We need divine wisdom to know how to unmask this cunning adversary. He constantly searches for ways to tempt and ensnare God's people. And in doing that he employs a double strategy: to entice them to sin, and then to accuse and condemn them for sinning. He is thoroughly acquainted with all their weaknesses and sins, and he accumulates them to solidify his case against them. "Satan has an accurate knowledge of the sins that he has tempted God's people to commit, and he urges his accusations against them, declaring that by their sins they have forfeited divine protection, and claiming that he has the right to destroy them" (*ibid.*, p. 588).

Our only hope is when Christ presents Himself as our substitute and surety, and He does. He lives to do His utmost to defend us, and in His love and mercy He places Himself in the firing line of Satan. Is not that enough of an incentive for us to shun sin? Do we not wish that we had not given our accuser so much ammunition so that he might build a better case against us and our Saviour? Are we giving him more ammunition today? What about tomorrow or next week? For the sake of Christ, and for our own eternal destiny, will we not submit ourselves to Him?

Will we not shun sin? How can we continue to be so reckless with our relationship with Him? How can we continue playing with sin, blinded to the unseen forces struggling constantly for our souls?

The Divine Defense. Joshua represents God's people in their desperate need for the ministry of Christ in their behalf. Christ and Satan contend over them as Satan claims them as his rightful possession. The accuser points to their sins as the reason that they should belong to him and not be restored to Christ. Their eternal destiny hangs in the balances. Satan tells the truth in his accusation, for they are guilty; and their only hope is found in Christ their defense and righteousness. Ellen White writes, "But He who was the hope of Israel then, their defense, their justification and redemption, is the hope of the church today" (*ibid.*, p. 585).

Jesus Christ is the antitype of Joshua as our advocate and high priest. "For our sake he [God] made him to be sin who knew no sin, so that in him we might become the righteousness of God" (2 Cor. 5:21). "And the Lord has laid on him [Christ] the iniquity of us all" (Isa. 53:6).

Rebuking Satan. The defense of Joshua was not a denial of guilt, rather it was a plea for sympathy and mercy. With Christ guilt is not dwelt upon when true confession and submission have taken place. He does not excuse Joshua's sins, nor does He apologize for him or ignore Joshua's filthy garments. But He is willing to confront Satan's accusations right in the open, and He silences him when He presents Himself as their sacrifice and covers them with His perfect righteousness. "The blood of Jesus Christ is the eloquent plea that speaks in behalf of sinners" (*Testimonies to Ministers*, p. 517).

How do we deal with Satan when he comes around to tempt us, bargain, and dispute with us? We are no match for Satan, but Christ is, and He offers us Himself and His victory in overcoming the tempter. Christ had several encounters with Satan besides this one in Zechariah 3. (See Jude 9 and

Luke 4:3, 4, 13, 35.) Christ, trusting in His Father, appealed to His word, and rebuked Satan.

Let us not be drawn to the allurements of the deceiver. We must make no deals with him. He is altogether the master of evil, but he is defeated and doomed, and he knows it. We need to unmask him with the light of God's love and truth. We must not get in combat with him, but just hand him over to "the Angel of the Lord." Our Advocate knows how to rebuke him and silence his accusations. "He [Jesus] pleads their cause, and by the *mighty* arguments of Calvary, vanquishes their accuser" (*Prophets and Kings*, p. 586; italics supplied).

Christ bases His defense of Joshua and His people on two points. The first relates to what He has done in their behalf. The second point in that defense has to do with the pitiful condition of Israel and their repentant attitude. In other words, the defense of their case was based on the Lord's initiative in choosing Jerusalem and on their response of repentance and surrender to Him as "a brand plucked from the fire" (Zech. 3:2). God's saving work and our response must always go together, hand in hand.

A Brand Plucked From the Fire. Have you ever thrown into the fire by mistake a precious letter, an important paper, or a rare document along with some waste paper? Then all of a sudden, to your horror, you discover that precious and irreplaceable piece of paper burning and almost consumed. Quickly you retrieve it in spite of the smoke and heat. You look at the burned page, protecting what is left. Sad that some of it was burned, but also glad that you saved a remnant of it before it was totally consumed.

If we feel this way about a piece of paper, imagine how Christ feels about His precious remnant people! The children of Israel passed through the fires of exile and persecution so that they were almost consumed by the flames. Satan would have kept them in the fiery flames to be utterly destroyed, but the merciful Lord intervened and brought back a few of His people as a precious remnant. Yes, the brand still spewed smoke, smelled of fire, and was disfigured; but He plucked them out of the fire just in time and did not want anyone to pluck them out of His hand.

It is, of course, shameful and low for Satan to bother with a brand that is already suffering enough and almost consumed. But that is Satan. He wants to snuff out any ray of hope or any glimmer of expectation from the struggling human heart. On the contrary, Christ fans any flickering hope, and lifts up the one who is down. Isaiah says of Him, "A bruised reed he will not break, and a dimly burning wick he will not quench" (Isa. 42:3).

Vindication and Restoration. The section of Joshua's experience with Christ recorded in Zechariah 3:4-8 encompasses the totality of salvation. Let us note the three phases: (1) *the covering*, symbolizing justification, (2) *walking here*, signifying sanctification, and (3) *walking there* among the angels in heaven, signifying glorification.

It is amazing that these few short verses summarize the whole plan of salvation shown in the person of Joshua — from a defiled person to a saint serving God in the courts of heaven! "He [Jesus] asks for His people not only pardon and justification, full and complete, but a share in His glory and a seat upon His throne" (*The Great Controversy*, p. 484).

The Covering. Christ asks the witnessing angels to take away Joshua's filthy garments, which symbolize his human righteousness, and then He addresses him saying, "Behold I have taken your iniquity away from you, and I will clothe you with rich apparel" (Zech. 3:4). It is interesting to note that the suggestion of the alert Zechariah to place "a clean turban" (verse 5) on Joshua's head was accepted. So the two articles of clothing placed on Joshua were the "rich apparel" and the "clean turban."

The theme of Christ covering us with His robe of righteousness is a powerful one in the Old Testament as well as the New.

Isaiah exclaims with great joy and exaltation because the Lord "has *clothed* me with the *garments of salvation*, he has *covered* me with the *robe of righteousness*" (Isa. 61:10).

Jeremiah relates a Messianic prophecy about the righteous Branch who will bring salvation and who will be called *"The Lord is our righteousness"* (Jer. 23:6). Compare this to the Branch mentioned in Zechariah 3:8, 9 who "will remove the guilt of this land in a single day."

And Paul declares of Christ, "He is the source of your life in Christ Jesus, whom God made our wisdom, our *righteousness* and sanctification and redemption" (1 Cor. 1:30).

Simply put, Christ is righteousness, and without Him there is not even a minute trace of righteousness. The righteousness we need for salvation always comes with Christ and never apart from Him. He offers Himself to us, and in receiving Him we receive His righteousness.

In commenting on this theme in Zechariah 3, Ellen White writes some gems of truth regarding Christ covering us with His robe of righteousness. "Israel was clothed with 'change of raiment' — the righteousness of Christ imputed to them" (*Prophets and Kings*, p. 584). "All who have put on the robe of Christ's righteousness will stand before Him as chosen and faithful and true. Satan has *no power* to pluck them out of the hand of the Saviour. *Not one soul* who in penitence and faith has claimed His protection will Christ permit to pass under the enemy's power" (*ibid.*, p. 587; italics supplied).

What does the "clean turban" placed on Joshua's head signify? The word *clean* in the Revised Standard Version, or *fair* in the King James Version, comes from the Hebrew word *ṭahar*, which means "to be clean," "to be pure," or "to be pronounced clean" or pure. In the Old Testament, the turban of the high priest had this inscription on it, "holiness to the Lord" (Ex. 28:36-38, KJV). By placing the pure turban on Joshua's head, the Lord was declaring him qualified to function as high priest in ministering before Him.

The pure robe and the pure turban placed on Joshua's body and head symbolize justification. But the pure turban may also signify sanctification, hence we have the commitment of heart and mind to Christ. With justification must always result "holiness to the Lord" — a sanctified life. For

Christ is not divided. He not only is our justification; He is also our sanctification (1 Cor. 1:30). "We cannot earn salvation, but we are to seek for it with as much interest and perseverance as though we would abandon everything in the world for it" (*Christ's Object Lessons*, p. 117).

With Christ's superb defense, Satan was completely silenced. He had run out of arguments, and it was his turn to be silenced for a change before the Lord's mighty defense. Yes, Satan can argue about human righteousness, but how could he argue against the perfect righteousness of Christ that covers the repentant sinner? "Christ *alone* can make an effectual plea in our behalf. He is able to silence the accuser with arguments founded *not upon our merits, but on His own*" (*Testimonies*, vol. 5, p. 472; italics supplied).

Walking With the Lord. It is plain from Zechariah 3:7 that being covered with the righteousness of Christ involves the experience of *walking* in and with Him. That involves walking in His ways and keeping His statutes. *Walking* is a word that signifies continuity, hence a life of continual sanctification in and with Christ. This is not necessarily hard work. It is rather heart work. Listen carefully to this profound statement, especially in terms of how to live for Christ. "All true obedience comes from the *heart*. It was heart work with Christ. And if we *consent*, He will so identify Himself with our thoughts and aims, so blend our hearts and minds into conformity to His will, that when obeying Him we shall be but carrying out our own impulses. . . . When we *know* God as it is our privilege to know Him, our life will be a life of *continual* obedience. Through an *appreciation* of the character of Christ, through *communion* with God, sin will become *hateful* to us" (*The Desire of Ages*, p. 668; italics supplied).

Walking There in Heaven. Salvation would not be complete without leaving this wicked world for the new world wherein dwells righteousness and where we will enjoy the abode of the angels who stand by Christ. Justification and sanctification through the righteousness of Christ will lead us most assuredly to glorification when the

Lord returns to take us unto Himself. What good news! Not only are the penalty and power of sin taken care of, but also the very presence of sin will be completely eradicated from this old world.

In Zechariah 3:7 we read: "Thus says the Lord of hosts: If you will walk in my ways and keep my charge, then you shall rule my house and have charge of my courts, and I will give you *the right of access among those who are standing here.*" If we are faithful to Christ to the end, He will give us free access to the heavenly courts to be with Him and all the angels forever.

I also find a secondary application here. We may walk among the angels in this world, too. After quoting the above text, Ellen White makes a double application, stating that if Joshua is obedient till the end, "he should join the glorified throng around the throne of God" (*Prophets and Kings*, p. 585). And "angels of God will walk on either side of them, even in this world, and they will stand at last among the angels that surround the throne of God" (*ibid.*, p. 587).

The complete fulfillment of Zechariah 3 is taking place now and will continue to take place in the future. Ellen White discusses the subject of the final vindication of God's people in the context of Joshua's experience. (See *The Great Controversy*, p. 484.) There is also an important reference to that in *The SDA Bible Commentary*: "It has been shown me that the experience recorded in the third chapter of Zechariah is now being acted over, and will continue to be while men, making profession of cleanness, refuse to humble the heart and confess their sins" (Ellen G. White Comments, vol. 4, p. 1179). And *Prophets and Kings*, page 591, alludes to the time when the people of God are sealed. Quoting Zechariah 3:4, she writes, "The despised remnant are clothed in glorious apparel, nevermore to be defiled by the corruptions of the world. . . . While Satan has been urging his accusations, holy angels, unseen, have been passing to and fro, placing upon the faithful ones the seal of the living God."

We are *now* living in the great day of atonement, and we *must* put on Christ and the robe of His righteousness. We *must* without any delay search our hearts to ascertain if we really have put on Christ. Some are confused as to what it means to be covered with Christ's righteousness. It is to our peril if we have any illusions or guesswork about this all-important matter. "When we *submit* ourselves to Christ, the heart is *united* with His heart, the will is *merged* in His will, the mind becomes one with His mind, the thoughts are brought into captivity to Him; *we live His life. This is what it means* to be clothed with the garment of His righteousness" (*Christ's Object Lessons*, p. 312; italics supplied).

Some people are treading on the dangerous ground of deadly presumption. They superficially accept the grace of Christ, and they wax eloquent discussing His wonderful righteousness that covers them, but they live not for Christ but for the world. They have a *form* of godliness, but deny its power (2 Tim. 3:5). "The righteousness of Christ will not cover one cherished sin" (*ibid.*, p. 316).

Our Advocate is "Jesus Christ *the righteous*" (1 John 2: 1), whose mighty intercession on our behalf avails much, but we must do our utmost to continually cleave to Him. If we choose not to center our lives around Christ, we are deciding in effect to separate ourselves from Him, and hence also separate ourselves from the covering of His righteousness. That would cause the greatest pain to the heart of our Redeemer. He draws us with cords of love and tells us that our salvation is found only in coming to Him and abiding in Him.

In this great controversy that is raging on between Christ and Satan for our souls, Christ our righteousness ever lives to make intercession for us; the devil lives to make accusations against us. We should have a "healthy respect" for Satan because we are no match for him. That is why James gave one of the most practical counsels in this regard. He writes, "*Submit* yourselves therefore to God. *Resist* the devil and he will *flee* from you" (James 4:7). Notice the order of these verbs in this verse: (1) submit, (2) resist, (3) flee. Before anything else, we need to submit ourselves to our Advocate so that we might be one with Him before resisting

Satan. As a result, Satan will do the fleeing in the face of our Saviour. That is the best and only way to live the abundant life here, to walk with Him on this earth as Enoch did, so that when He comes in the clouds His coming will not be a surprise to us, and we will continue to walk with Him forever in His glory.

By
His Spirit

Some years ago I had the opportunity to attend a camp meeting with the important theme of "O Come, Holy Spirit!" as the focus of every evening's meeting. I remember being excited about the subject of receiving the Holy Spirit into our lives and looking forward to these meetings with great anticipation. To my disappointment, however, the meetings for each evening that week dealt with how not to receive the wrong spirit, instead of how to receive the right Spirit. We were so cautioned about the dangers of emotionalism and counterfeits that we somehow missed out on what the theme "O Come, Holy Spirit!" seemed to imply.

Of course, we need to be cautious about counterfeits, especially in these last days of spiritual confusion, but not to the extent that we don't obtain from God what is genuine. In other words, in trying not to get the wrong experience, we may miss receiving the right experience of the Holy Spirit. That indeed would be tragic.

Perhaps our lack of acquaintance with the third person of the Godhead lies behind this ambivalence. We feel more at ease with Christ our Saviour. Christ seems more real to us, so we can identify with Him. Maybe the use of the term *spirit* to describe Him gives some the impression that He is something ethereal—a power or influence, not a real person like Christ. In this chapter we will study the Holy Spirit in the context of Zechariah 4, and see how He paints a beautiful portrait of the Messiah.

So far we have concentrated more specifically on God

the Father and God the Son at work, but now we shall focus on God the Holy Spirit. The Holy Spirit has a personality as real as the Father and the Son. The Bible clearly presents Him as someone who functions in the capacity of a person. He is not an idea or an influence—He is a person. He teaches (Luke 12:12), comforts and convicts (John 16:7, 8, 15; 14:26), and sanctifies (1 Peter 1:2). The closeness of the Father and the Son to the Holy Spirit is evident by the designation of the Spirit as both "the Spirit of God" and "the Spirit of Christ" in the same verse in Romans 8:9. In Zechariah 4:6 He is called the Spirit of the Lord of hosts.

The work of the Holy Spirit is linked together with Christ's life and ministry. He was a close companion to Christ from the very beginning. Christ was conceived of the Holy Spirit (Matt. 1:20) and anointed by the Spirit at His baptism, thus commencing Jesus' public ministry (John 1:32-34). The Holy Spirit was sent to fill Christ's place as the *other* Comforter, and so He is among us as Christ's personal representative (John 14:16-26). He does not speak on His own authority, but He bears witness to Christ and glorifies Him (John 16:13, 14; 15:26). Finally, in the Holy Spirit Christ comes to us, because the Spirit dwells with us and is in us (John 14:17, 18).

Just as we learned in the previous chapter that the righteousness of Christ was essential, efficient, and sufficient for Joshua the high priest, so we shall learn in this chapter that the Holy Spirit, who is the Spirit of Christ, is also essential and sufficient for Zerubbabel, the governor of Judah.

In Zechariah 4 as in Zechariah 3 there are also two central figures. The central *human* figure is Zerubbabel, and the central *divine* Figure is the Holy Spirit. The theme of chapter 4 is the Holy Spirit, symbolized by the oil that empowered Zerubbabel to accomplish God's will as the leader of His people. And just as the oil of the two olive trees replenishes the lampstand, so also the oil of the Holy Spirit supplies the power for Zerubbabel. This central theme is evident from the response of the angel to Zechariah's inquiry as to what *all* the things that he saw meant. "This is the word of the Lord to Zerubbabel: Not by might, nor by power, but *by my Spirit*, says the Lord of hosts" (Zech. 4:6).

Moreover, Zechariah 4 complements and reinforces Zechariah 3 and is essential to it. The great experience of receiving and living Christ's righteousness in chapter 3 must be maintained by the empowering ministry of the Holy Spirit in chapter 4. It is so true that in order to keep the righteousness of Christ, we must maintain our walk with Him from day to day. For such an experience to continue and flourish, it must depend on the unending flow and sharing of the Holy Spirit in and through our lives. We keep the robe of Christ's righteousness not by our human might, but by *His Spirit*.

Zerubbabel. The Scriptures shed a fair amount of light on the life and work of Zerubbabel. Let us look briefly at this great man whom God used to lead His people in rebuilding the Temple during very trying circumstances.

1. Zerubbabel had descended from the royal line of King David (1 Chron. 3:19).

2. He was a prince and a governor of Judah (Ezra 1:8 and Haggai 2:21). He was given the Babylonian name of "Shesh-bazzar" in Ezra 1:8.

3. He was appointed to the important position of being the leader of the returned exiles from their Babylonian captivity (Neh. 7:6, 7).

4. He was the first political leader to restore the worship of God in Jerusalem after the Jewish remnant had returned from exile in Babylon (Ezra 3:8).

5. He was the political leader who completed the rebuilding of the Temple against many odds, internal and external. The returned exiles were discouraged, and their enemies severely opposed them. The prophecy in Zechariah 4:9, 10 relating to finishing the rebuilding of the Temple was actually fulfilled according to Ezra 6:14, 15 during the sixth year of Darius' reign.

6. He was an ancestor of Christ the Messiah (Matt. 1:12; Luke 3:27).

7. Finally, Zerubbabel was a type of Christ as God's Servant and Branch (Haggai 2:23; Zech. 6:12, 13). This comparison is fitting, because Christ was also empowered with the Holy Spirit to restore the temple of God's presence in the human heart.

Study the following drawing of all the things Zechariah saw in his fifth vision. Then note very carefully the following items numbered on the drawing, because both the drawing and this list will prove useful in helping us understand the important implications of the vision:

1. A golden lampstand with seven lamps.

2. A bowl above the lampstand.

3. Each one of the seven smaller pipes leading from the bowl to each one of the seven lamps.

4. Each one of the two bigger golden pipes leading from each of the two olive trees to the bowl above the lampstand.

5. The two olive trees, the source of the golden oil, transmit the oil through the two bigger golden pipes to the bowl, and from the bowl the golden oil is transmitted to the seven lamps through the seven smaller pipes.

Four major symbols appear in Zechariah's fifth vision: the two olive trees, the lampstand, the oil, and the light. A logical sequence of these symbols is seen here. However, it may be preferable to study them in the order they follow in the vision and in its interpretation.

The Golden Lampstand—The symbolism of the lampstand (or candlestick) comes from the ancient tabernacle, which had seven lamps and was made from one mold of pure gold (Ex. 25:31-40). The lampstand Zechariah saw in vision has the same symbolic origin, and here in the context of chapter 4 it has its own specific applications. Here it mainly points to Zerubbabel, the central human figure, who is supplied with the golden oil of the Holy Spirit from the two olive trees, which empowers him to do God's work at hand. He needs the Holy Spirit to rebuild the Temple, and he receives Him just as the lampstand receives the golden oil supplied by the olive trees.

Another contextual evidence that the lampstand symbolizes Zerubbabel is the response of the angel to Zechariah's question "What are these?" (Zech. 4:4), referring to the lampstand and the olive trees. It is addressed directly to Zerubbabel himself: "This is the word of the Lord to Zerubbabel: Not by might, nor by power, but by my Spirit, says the Lord of hosts" (verse 6). God seems to be saying, "Zerubbabel, you cannot rebuild the Temple by your own human might, by your own empty lamp; but you can rebuild it by what you see in the vision: the golden oil of the Holy Spirit flowing through the lamp of your life and giving you light and power to accomplish the urgent task at hand of rebuilding the Temple."

Notice the following diagram:

1. The Olive Trees   Supplier of Oil   to the Lampstand

2. The Holy Spirit   Supplier of Light/Power   to Zerubbabel

Ellen G. White uses the term *lamp* to point to the life of the individual. She makes several references, in the context of Zechariah 4, to the golden oil of the Holy Spirit in the lamp of a person's heart to give him light and power. For example: "Each person has his own light to keep burning; and if the heavenly oil is emptied into these *lamps* through the golden pipes; if the vessels are emptied of self, and prepared to receive the holy oil, light will be shed" (*Testimonies*, vol. 6, p. 116; italics supplied).

The lampstand is completely dependent on the golden oil of the two olive trees to burn and give light. In a sense, we ourselves are lampstands, or as Jesus said to His disciples and to us, "You are the light of the world" (Matt. 5:14). However, our light becomes darkness without Jesus, who Himself is "the light of the world" (John 8:12). And Paul writes, "For once you were darkness, but now you are light in the Lord; walk as children of light" (Eph. 5:8).

King David, the ancestor of Governor Zerubbabel, was also referred to in the Bible as "the lamp of Israel" (2 Sam. 21:17). But then a chapter later David acknowledges that God is the lamp: "Yea, thou art my lamp, O Lord, and my God lightens my darkness" (2 Sam. 22:29). Another example is found in Jesus' parable of the five wise and five foolish virgins (Matt. 25:1-13). The lamps of the wise virgins, which were supplied with oil, symbolized their lives full of the Spirit's light and power. However, the lamps of the foolish virgins, which had no oil, symbolized their lives devoid of that same light and power. "The wise [virgins] took oil in their vessels with their lamps. This is the holy oil represented in Zechariah [Zech. 4:11-14 quoted]. . . . The oil is received into the vessels prepared for the oil. It is the Holy Spirit in the heart which works by love and purifies the soul" (*The SDA Bible Commentary*, Ellen G. White Comments, vol. 4, p. 1179).

It is apparent from the above examples that David,

Zerubbabel, the disciples of Christ, the wise virgins, and we all may be symbolized by lights or lamps glowing with God's light and power. But no matter how sophisticated and talented we may be, unless our human lamps are fueled by the holy oil of the Spirit of Christ, we become darkness, lamps without the flame. "Humanity has in itself no light. Apart from Christ we are like an unkindled taper, like the moon when her face is turned away from the sun; we have not a single ray of brightness to shed into the darkness of the world. But when we turn toward the Sun of Righteousness, when we come in touch with Christ, the whole soul is aglow with the brightness of the divine presence" (*Thoughts From the Mount of Blessing*, p. 40).

O Great Mountain!—Zerubbabel faced many difficult challenges and obstacles thrust upon him from within and from without, and they all undermined the progress of rebuilding the Temple. The people became worried about material prosperity and neglected building God's house. Only a minority of the Jews returned from Babylon—about 50,000, which led to discouragement, especially when the older ones remembered with anguished regret the former glory of the Temple. The Samaritans also afforded a constant source of irritation and persecution—a thorn in the flesh.

Discouragement can be one of the most difficult mountains to face, and when coupled with outside ridicule and persecution, it can become devastating. Discouragement can be especially demoralizing and debilitating when we allow ourselves to focus on whatever is discouraging, and so look away from Christ. Discouragement can lead to disillusionment, which can lead to despair; and despair can lead to disaster. But we must not give in to discouragement—one of Satan's most devastating weapons. We must look away from ourselves to Christ. "Throughout the history of God's people great mountains of difficulty, apparently insurmountable, have loomed up before those who were trying to carry out the purposes of Heaven" (*Prophets and Kings*, p. 594). "While we realize our hopeless condition without Christ, we are *not to yield* to discouragement, but rely upon the merits of a crucified and risen Saviour. Look and Live" (*Patriarchs and Prophets*, p. 432; italics supplied). "Talk and act as if your faith was *invincible*" (*Christ's Object Lessons*, p. 147; italics supplied).

Zerubbabel could have easily slipped into discouragement and given up, but he allowed the Holy Spirit to fill him—to empower him to see great mountains leveled. The hands of Zerubbabel finished rebuilding the Temple (Zech. 4:9), and the headstone was brought to celebrate its completion (verse 7; see also Ezra 6:14, 15).

Jesus, as an antitype of Zerubbabel, was filled with and empowered by the Holy Spirit to meet victoriously the great mountains of Satan's temptations in the wilderness and throughout His ministry. Satan could not make Him deviate from building His temple in human hearts through the Holy Spirit. He certainly faced mountains much greater than Zerubbabel or anyone of us have ever had to face. He well knows our struggles and is able to sympathize with us. "As the world's Redeemer, Christ was *constantly confronted with apparent failure*. He seemed to do little of the work which He longed to do in uplifting and saving. Satanic agencies were constantly working to obstruct His way. *But He would not be discouraged*" (*Gospel Workers*, p. 514; italics supplied). Can we identify with Christ in this?

We have learned that Zerubbabel *completed* rebuilding the Temple. Notice that he did not just start it, but he also finished it. Some people are very efficient in starting new projects, but very inefficient in completing them. How many countless programs have been launched with great noise and excitement only to run out of steam and falter into oblivion!

It takes commitment and discipline on our part as well as the enabling power of the Spirit to persevere and successfully complete the tasks that He calls us to do. The Holy Spirit leads us not to focus so much on the "great mountains," but more important, on His power in making such great mountains level plains. He is a beginner *and* a finisher. He not only initiates a project, but He also completes it. You and I are His special projects, and "he who began a good work in you will bring it to completion at the day of Jesus Christ" (Phil. 1:6).

Robert H. Schuller tells us in his "Credo for Possibility Thinkers" what we can do when confronted with a mountain. "When faced with a mountain, I will not quit. I will keep on striving until I climb over it, find a path through it, tunnel under it, or simply stay and turn the mountain into a gold mine—with God's help."

The Day of Small Things—A story is told about the building of St. Paul's Cathedral in London during World War II. One day a visitor came by to look at the progress of the construction. As he looked around, he saw one worker moving debris from one area to another, and he stopped and asked him what he was doing. The man disgruntledly responded by saying that he was moving dirt from here to there. The visitor saw another laborer doing exactly the same kind of work, and he asked him the same question. With a sense of pride this second worker responded that he was helping build the great Cathedral of St. Paul.

Both men were doing the same work, seemingly unimportant, yet each of them viewed the situation quite differently. How do we view our days of seemingly small things? Are we just moving dirt, or are we helping in the important work of building the kingdom of God?

Zerubbabel, the new governor of a small group of returned Jewish exiles, knew well "the day of small things" mentioned in Zechariah 4:10. He also discerned through all the small beginnings God's great plan for restoring His people unto Himself. God's program might seem insignificant sometimes, but it would triumph through the power of the Holy Spirit.

This Temple was not as great as the first one. The human and material resources were now more limited than during the reign of Solomon. The returned exiles often grew discouraged when they compared their "day of small things" with the great days of King Solomon. They had to rebuild the beautiful Temple of Solomon from rubble, which required a lot of patience and delay, and doing a host of seemingly small things. But God saw things differently, for He declared that "the latter splendor of this house shall be greater than the former" (Haggai 2:9). God was to fill it with His glory, and Christ would grace it with His presence during His first advent. That certainly was much greater than any grand building they could have built. Even Solomon's Temple was not honored with the physical presence of the incarnate Son of God.

Christ speaks—often unnoticed—in a "still small voice" (1 Kings 19:12) through His Holy Spirit. He used a powerful example when He talked about the great potential of one of the tiniest seeds—a mustard seed—that became a giant bush (Mark 4:30-32). He also said, "He who is faithful in *a very little* is faithful also in much" (Luke 16:10).

You've heard the popular saying "bigger is better," haven't you? And because we sometimes think that way, we tend to despise the day of small things. We often want things to be big, impressive—and we want them *now*. But God often does not work that way. The big events in our lives often start with and result from small beginnings. The big day often results from many ordinary days. The history of the world is full of great events that started from seemingly insignificant things. Who can estimate the value of a genuine smile, a friendly gesture, a firm handshake, or a kind word?

"The way of the world is to begin with pomp and boasting. God's way is to make the day of small things the beginning of the glorious triumph of truth and righteousness" (*Prophets and Kings*, p. 595). "The church seem content to take only the first steps in conversion. They are more ready for active labor than for humble devotion, more ready to engage in outward religious service than in the inner work of the heart. Meditation and prayer are neglected for bustle and show" (*Testimonies*, vol. 4, p. 535).

The Two Olive Trees and the Golden Oil—The olive tree plays an important part in feeding and providing a livelihood for many Mediterranean countries. It has done so since ancient time, especially around Palestine. Olives and the oil extracted from them have been for many centuries a vital food staple in that part of the world. The oil extracted from the olive tree has many uses; it also holds rich symbolism in the Bible. Such uses include: for food (Num. 11:8), for anointing (1 Sam. 10:1), for illumination (Ex. 25:6; Matt. 25:3-8), and for beautification (Ruth 3:3). It also symbolizes prosperity (Deut. 32:13), brotherly love (Ps. 133:2), joy (Isa. 61:3), and the Holy Spirit (Matt. 25:4; 1 John 2:20, 27).

Zechariah asked three times about the two olive trees, and received two answers from the interpreting angel (Zech. 4:4-6, 11-14). In responding to his first question, the angel specifically pointed to the Holy Spirit: "Not by might, nor by power, but by my spirit" (verse 6, KJV). But then the angel responded to the last two questions by saying that the two olive trees "are the two anointed who stand by the Lord of the whole earth" (verse 14). The "two anointed" literally mean, "the two sons of oil." From the context, it is seen that they *furnish* the golden oil, but do *not receive* it. The expression "two sons of oil" in Hebrew can mean suppliers of oil—originators of it. "So from the holy ones that stand in God's presence, His Spirit is imparted to human instrumentalities that are consecrated to His service. The mission of the two anointed ones is to communicate light and power to God's people" (*Testimonies to Ministers*, p. 510).

The angel does not explain precisely who these two anointed ones are. But the implication is clear from the context, and it follows logically that they represent the Spirit of God mentioned in Zechariah 4:6 and His divine agencies. They are identified as the source of the golden oil awaiting instructions from "the Lord of the whole earth" (verse 14). They are as representative of the Spirit of God as the two olive trees (verse 6) and serve the same important function. And just as they replenish the lampstand with the golden oil, so also the Holy Spirit gives of Himself to us. Therefore, these important symbols—the two olive trees, the two anointed ones, and the golden oil—all represent the same person, the Holy Spirit.

It is interesting to note that the lampstand is being fed

by the two olive trees, or the two sons of oil, but not by any human hand. This is significant because the golden oil of the Spirit of God is not supplied by any human effort, but is supplied purely by the inexhaustible and unfailing store-house of God. The supply is limitless and flows continu-ously and freely as the Spirit wills. There is absolutely no trace of human effort or manipulation in this; it is all the work of God. "In the work of God, humanity can originate *nothing*. No man can by his own effort make himself a light bearer for God" (*Christ's Object Lessons*, p. 418; italics supplied). "We need to have far less confidence in what man can do and far more confidence in what God can do for every believing soul" (*ibid.*, p. 146).

Not by Might, Nor by Power—It is clear to us so far that Zerubbabel did not accomplish the rebuilding of the Tem-ple in his own might or by human effort, but by the divine might of God's Spirit. Now we need to ask ourselves this important question: What is the might of God's Spirit in Zechariah 4:6? The usual interpretation of this well-known text is something like this, "not by man's might, but by God's might," instead of "not by man's might, but by God's Spirit." There is a way of looking at this text that goes beyond God's great power to the power of His Spirit of love and mercy. He would rather always deal lovingly with people, and not resort to sheer force as the first measure.

Satan prefers to use force and violence. For him might makes right, but for God right makes might. Satan does not have any truth or righteousness on his side, but God does. It is frequently true that when individuals, groups, or nations do not have the right and the truth on their side, they tend to use force and coercion in dealing with others as an acceptable way of behavior. In essence, this is a telling sign of weakness and not of true strength. They *have* to use force because they have nothing else going for them.

Consider the example of Jesus. When He made His triumphal entry to Jerusalem riding on an ass (Zech. 9:9), He showed that He was "meek and lowly in heart." A donkey symbolized meekness, humility, and peace. Jesus was not victorious by riding on a horse, or in a chariot using the power of the sword. Jesus will ultimately win the great controversy not just because He is more powerful, but because He is truth and love personified.

The Holy Spirit is likewise the "Spirit of truth" (John 14:17), and the "Spirit of Jesus Christ" (Phil. 1:19), who testifies and gives glory to Christ (John 16:13, 14). Jesus told His disciples that "it is to your advantage that I go away, for if I do not go away, the Counselor will not come to you; but if I go, I will send him to you" (verse 7). The man Jesus in His incarnation was not omnipresent, but He is now present everywhere through His Holy Spirit. In this connection it is enlightening to look at Zechariah 4:10, which says: "These seven are the eyes of the Lord, which range through the whole earth."

There is a close and intimate relationship between Christ and the Holy Spirit, so these seven eyes may refer primarily to the Holy Spirit, but also they may refer to Christ, or to both. The number seven symbolizes perfection. And the oil in the seven lamps of the lampstand in the Temple was positioned in seven directions, symbolizing the all-encompassing presence and power of the Holy Spirit throughout the whole earth, testifying of and glorifying Christ. Of course, the oil in the seven lamps represents the Holy Spirit. However, in Revelation 5:6 the seven eyes of the Lamb also represent the Spirit of God going into all the earth. These all-seeing, all-knowing, and all-present eyes of God never slumber nor sleep (Ps. 121:4), and they "range throughout the earth to strengthen those whose hearts are fully committed to him" (2 Chron. 16:9, NIV).

In conclusion, let us again consider the questions raised in the introduction regarding our reception of the Holy Spirit, but this time in light of these inspired statements: "But should the Lord work upon men as He did on and after the day of Pentecost, many who now claim to believe the truth . . . would cry, 'Beware of fanaticism.' . . . There will be those who will question and criticize when the Spirit of God takes possession of men and women, because their own hearts are not moved, but are cold and unimpressible" (*Selected Messages*, book 2, p. 57).

"This promise [of the Holy Spirit] belongs as much to us as it did to them [the disciples], and yet how *rarely* it is presented before the people, and its reception spoken of in the church. . . . The promise of the Holy Spirit is *casually* brought into our discourses, is *incidentally* touched upon, and that is all. . . . This subject has been *set aside*, as if some time in the future would be given to its consideration. . . . This promised blessing, if claimed by faith, would bring all other blessings in its train. . . . The power of God awaits their demand and reception" (*Testimonies to Ministers*, pp. 174, 175; italics supplied).

"Why do we not hunger and thirst for the gift of the Spirit, since this is the means by which we are to receive power? Why do we not talk of it, pray for it, preach concerning it?" (*Testimonies*, vol. 8, p. 22).

Christ
the Judge

What thoughts and feelings are conjured up in your mind when the subject of judgment is mentioned or discussed in your presence? It all depends on how one views the judgment and what he associates with it. Some of us may try to ignore the subject, but it is inescapable because "we must *all* appear before the judgment seat of Christ" (2 Cor. 5:10).

We often follow court trials with great interest, anticipating the outcome and hoping that the truth will be known, the innocent vindicated, and the guilty punished. And when the outcome is fair, we all breathe a sigh of relief and satisfaction, knowing that everything turned out all right. We ourselves would want to have "our day in court" and appear before a fair judge were we falsely accused of a serious crime. We would be very anxious to be vindicated—having the case tried and the truth known.

If we then take so much interest in earthly tribunals, why don't we take as much interest, if not more, in the heavenly tribunal, which will deal specifically with our cases and determine our eternal destiny? We must not be hesitant to acquaint ourselves with this crucial subject of the judgment. The popular saying that what we don't know does not hurt us implies that what we do know may hurt us. We can turn this proverb around and say that knowing the facts about God's judgment is indeed good news. And it is so because of the kind of judge we have in Jesus Christ.

Later in this chapter we will review the biblical meaning of the word *judgment*, but for now we shall focus on Christ our judge. According to the Bible, God the Father is the judge, so how and why is Christ also the judge? Jesus Himself gives the answer to both questions. How: "The Father . . . has given all judgment to the Son" (John 5:22). Why: "[The Father] has *given* him [Christ] authority to execute judgment, because he is *the Son of man*" (verse 27).

Christ is uniquely qualified to be the judge, because He is the Son of God and also the Son of man. He was tempted in all things, vicariously became sin for us, tasted death, and triumphed over Satan. So He can adequately sympathize with humanity while vindicating His Father. Our Judge has great credentials. He knows us and is acquainted with all our circumstances; He is our Creator; He is our Saviour; He is our advocate; He is our high priest; He is our righteousness, justification, and sanctification; and He is the complete embodiment of all truth, fairness, virtue, understanding, and mercy. He, in His immeasurable love, gave His life on the cross for us. Thank God for such a judge as we have in Christ!

Christ's primary task is to save us. That is why He came to this world. Even in His function as the judge, His great love is manifested not only to the righteous, but also to the wicked, who spurn His mercy. "He [Christ] who has followed the soul with tenderest entreaty, seeking to win it from sin to holiness, is in one its advocate and judge. . . . It is He who has encountered the deceiver, and who through all the ages has been seeking to wrest the captives from his grasp, who will pass judgment upon every soul. . . . [He] will deal justly and tenderly with the souls that His own blood has been poured out to save—because of this, the Son of man is appointed to execute the judgment" (*The Desire of Ages*, p. 210).

In this chapter, we will study Zechariah's sixth and seventh visions in the context of judgment and vindication. The judgment of God is all-pervasive. It will affect all: the individual, Israel, and the world—to either condemn those who reject salvation or to vindicate those who accept and live salvation. However, in the scope of our study, we will deal only with God's judgment regarding His people. It is evident that God wants to eradicate sin from the hearts of His people and from the whole earth. The time will come when He will do just that.

Additionally, this chapter should be read in the context of the previous chapters, because it serves as a continuation or a complement to them. As we have seen already, the Lord wants to return to us, to dwell in our midst, to cover us with His righteousness, and to empower us with His Holy Spirit. What more can He do! He is totally committed to us. But one thing He cannot do. He cannot—will not—force His will on us.

Let us look briefly at the following outline of Zechariah 5:1–6:8.

The Flying Roll	The Woman in the Ephah	The Four Chariots
The Sixth Vision	**The Seventh Vision**	**The Eighth Vision**
Judgment—	Judgment—	Judgment—
The Individual	Israel	The Nations
(5:1-4)	(5:5-11)	(6:1-8)

The experience of Joshua's vindication and restoration in the fourth vision resulted from Christ's gift of mercy and robe of righteousness. It also resulted because of Joshua's genuine repentance. That court scene, in a sense, continues in our day. Are we now accepting and appropriating with all our hearts what Christ has done for us? Is the Holy Spirit filling our lives and enabling us to walk in Him? But if we respond by turning away from Him, rejecting His robe of righteousness, grieving His Holy Spirit, and choosing to persist in separating ourselves from Him, then what else can He do?

"The righteous will continually follow righteousness, because Christ, who is formed within, is righteousness and truth. . . . He will give all needed help to those who call upon Him for strength for the development of Christlike character. But His love is not weakness. He will not serve with their sins. . . . Only through faithful repentance will their sins be forgiven; for God will not cover evil with the robe of His righteousness" (Ellen G. White, in *Signs of the Times*, Nov. 13, 1901).

It is the Christlike character and the fruits of the Holy Spirit in our lives which really demonstrate that we are one with Christ. Our profession is not necessarily an expression of our character, and it is that character formed within through our union with Christ that determines our eternal destiny. If He remains in our lives as the center of our existence, then we will be vindicated and will live with Him for eternity. But if sin instead of Christ resides within us, and we continue to cling to it, then we will have to face the judgment without the covering of Christ. We will be left at the mercy of the law and sin. The law will condemn us and sin will consume us. To abide in Christ is vindication and life eternal, and to abide in sin is condemnation and death.

The Vision of the Flying Scroll. The roll, or scroll, that Zechariah saw in this sixth vision had the measurements of about 17 by 34 feet. In Bible times, often the scrolls used for writing were made out of leather. Sometimes the writings on a scroll indicated cursings and judgment, as in Deuteronomy 29:20. When we compare this verse with Zechariah 5:3, 4 we discover some judgment terminology in both, such as "curses . . . would settle upon," "blot out his name from under heaven," "cut off," and "enter the house . . . and consume it, both timber and stones." Do not the last words sound very much like the words of judgment pronounced on the evildoers in Malachi 4:1? "For behold, the day comes, burning like an oven, when all the arrogant and all evildoers will be stubble; the day that comes shall burn them up . . . so that it will leave them neither root nor branch."

The scroll was not concealed in some obscure corner of the Temple for just the priests to glance at, but it was flung publicly across the face of the land of Judah to be seen by everyone. So also with the judgment of God. Zechariah must have seen the scroll open to have figured its dimensions. These large dimensions indicate the magnitude of the curse over the whole land. Also, these measurements are the same as those of the porch of Solomon's Temple. Perhaps they may imply some connection between the flying scroll and the Temple porch, especially when considering that they both contain a judgment motif. And we know that judgment proceeds from the Temple of God.

The interpreting angel calls this flying scroll "the curse that goes out over the face of the whole land" (Zech. 5:3) actively doing its assigned work. The scroll with writing suggests judgment and condemnation. It also points to the law of God, which becomes a curse and condemnation to every person under it and not under the blood of Christ. This is also implied in the context, because the curse comes against those who steal and those who bear false witness—two representative commandments of the law in Exodus 20. Without Christ, Paul found that the law proved death to him (Rom. 7:7-25).

So we have before us salvation in Christ's righteousness. Otherwise, if we do not have that, then we are left under the full weight of the demands of the law, which condemns and destroys us. Those who refuse Christ and do not appropriate in their lives the "change of raiment," the robe of His righteousness, and reject being nourished by the "golden oil" of the Spirit are condemned by the law of God.

Ellen G. White writes this applicable and strong statement after quoting Zechariah 5:1-4. This statement is to be understood in its correct context of the flying scroll condemning the rejecters of God's mercy. "Against every evil-doer God's law utters condemnation. He may disregard that voice, he may seek to drown its warning, but in vain. It follows him. It makes itself heard. It destroys his peace. If unheeded, it pursues him to the grave. It bears witness against him at the judgment. A quenchless fire, it consumes at last soul and body" (*Education*, pp. 144, 145).

So how do we avoid the law's curse and condemnation? We do that simply by continual adherence to Christ. If the previous statement from the book *Education* is the consequence of repudiating Christ's righteousness, then this fitting statement from *Steps to Christ*, pages 62, 63, is Jesus' "way of escape" from the condemnation of the law. "We have no righteousness of our own with which to meet the claims of the law of God. But Christ has made a way of escape for us. . . . He lived a sinless life. He died for us, and now He offers to take our sins and give us His righteousness. If you give yourself to Him, and accept Him as your Saviour, then, sinful as your life may have been, for His sake you are accounted righteous. Christ's character stands in place of your character. . . . More than this, Christ changes the heart. He abides in your heart by faith. You are to maintain this connection with Christ by faith and the continual surrender of your will to Him; and so long as you do this, He will work in you to will and to do according to His good pleasure."

God loves His sinful people but hates to see them cling to their deadly sins. He abhors sin and greatly desires to rid His people of it. A physician is not against his patients; he is against their fatal disease. He wants to rid them of it and save their lives. However, if they decline his offer, that disease will eventually kill them. Our great Physician longs to rid us of sin, but if we insist on holding on to our cherished sin and persist in rejecting Him, then He utters these words of anguished love, "How can I give you up, O Ephraim!" (Hosea 11:8), and "Ephraim is joined to idols, let him alone" (Hosea 4:17).

The twofold mission of the flying scroll in Zechariah 5:3 is to descend on two types of individuals: (1) Everyone who steals—the thief and (2) everyone who swears falsely—the perjurer. These two sins may be compared with the eighth and ninth commandments of the Decalogue. We perhaps ask ourselves why these particular sins were condemned. In a sense, these two commandments are quite representative of those commandments in Exodus 20 that pertain to our love to our fellowmen. The sin of stealing is committed against one's fellowman, but those who swear falsely in God's name commit a sin not only against man but also against God. This sin of perjury is something hidden and maybe known by God alone. This sin of the heart has to do with obstructing justice and being passive in defending or revealing the truth.

Stealing and swearing falsely were the two prevalent sins among the returned exiles, and their condemnation reveals that God is concerned about the ethical behavior of His people. Excellent theology has been presented so far, but now we are dealing with ethical and practical issues. All good theology must be followed by ethical imperatives, and ethics must be based on sound theology. These ethical questions are raised here only after God's gifts of forgiveness, righteousness, and His Spirit were presented. Such gifts accepted and appropriated naturally lead us to live godly lives.

Perhaps the main expression for crime in an economically strapped nation is stealing and swearing falsely. There were individuals who possibly held on to land and would not give it to their rightful owners when they returned from exile. Then there were those who obstructed justice, who were perjurers, and who lied secretly in their hearts. Maybe their secret sins were not known by others, but God knew everything. "Sin may be concealed, denied, covered up from father, mother, wife, children, and associates; no one but the guilty actors may cherish the least suspicion of the wrong; but it is laid bare before the intelligence of heaven. . . . He [God] is not deceived by appearances of piety. . . . Men may be deceived by those who are corrupt in heart, but God pierces all disguises and reads the inner life" (*The Great Controversy*, p. 486). God also "will bring to light the hidden things of darkness, and will make manifest the counsels of the hearts" (1 Cor. 4:5, KJV).

Jesus in His Sermon on the Mount deals with this subject by probing deep into the motives of our actions. He goes beyond the letter of the law to the heart of the law. For example, we say that we have the truth. By that we generally mean that we possess correct teachings. That is true, but having the truth is more than that. It means to tell the truth—to be truthful in our words and motives. To mean what we say, and say what we mean. To be people of our word. To have the truth means not being double-faced. In today's society, committing a crime is often not what people worry about. Rather, they worry lest they get caught in the act. And what they feel disappointed about is that they were not wily enough to cover their tracks.

The two sins we have been discussing are mentioned in relationship with specific individuals, namely the thief and the perjurer (Zech. 5:3). These types of individuals, who apparently did not appropriate God's gifts of mercy, stand under the full weight of the law to be condemned by the flying scroll. The expression "cut off" is usually associated with judgment and condemnation in the Old Testament. It is used here and also in the same context in Leviticus 23:29 in association with the Day of Atonement. Notice how in Leviticus it also refers to specific individuals: "For *any person* who is not afflicted of soul on that same day [day of atonement], he shall be *cut off* from his people" (NKJV). This was a very solemn day when the people of God searched their hearts, confessed their sins, and placed themselves at the mercy of God. The high priest entered the Most Holy Place with the blood of the sin offering and sprinkled it upon the mercy seat, which was located above the tables of the law (Lev. 16:15).

Thus mercy and justice met each other, and the blood of the Lamb of God slain from the foundation of the world (Rev. 13:8) satisfied the infinite demands of God's law. Christ is not only our judge, but He is also our high priest and sacrifice. His blood (the gift of His life) justifies us (Rom. 5:9). It also redeems us (Eph. 1:7; Heb. 9:12) and cleanses us from all sin (1 John 1:7). This precious blood sprinkled on the law of God met the penalty of death and satisfied the requirements of justice (Rom. 6:23; 3:26) on behalf of repentant sinners. It also frees them from the law's curse and condemnation. This freedom came at a high price. Christ on the cross bore upon Himself the full penalty of our transgression of the law and its condemnation. "By the offering of blood, the sinner acknowledged the *authority of the law*, confessed the guilt of his transgression, and expressed his faith in Him who was to take away the sin of the world. . . . On the Day of Atonement, the high priest having taken an offering for the congregation, went into the Most Holy Place with the blood and sprinkled it upon the mercy seat, above the tables of the law. *Thus the claims of the law, which demanded the life of the sinner, were satisfied"* (*Patriarchs and Prophets*, p. 356; italics supplied).

We must bear in mind that God's primary desire and first priority during the Day of Atonement was not the condemnation of His people but their vindication. In His judgment God wants to do something positive *for* His people and not something negative *against* them. His judgment is negative only if we insist on having it so by our continual rejection of His offers of mercy. He simply honors our choice.

This is consistent with the original and literal meaning of the word *atonement* in the expression "Day of Atonement." The Hebrew word for atonement is *kippurîm*, which means "a covering," from the Hebrew verb *kaphar*, which means "to cover." We can see a connection between the atonement as Christ covering our confessed and forsaken sins and the offer of His perfect robe of righteousness in Zechariah 3:4 to cover our spiritual nakedness.

Christ uses the expression "the wedding garment" in one of His parables to describe His robe of righteousness (Matt. 22:1-14). Ellen G. White comments on this important parable in the context of the antitypical Day of Atonement. "It is while men are still dwelling upon the earth that the work of investigative judgment takes place in the courts of heaven. . . . By the wedding garment in the parable is represented the pure, spotless character which Christ's true followers will possess. . . . Only the *covering* which Christ Himself has provided can make us meet to appear in God's presence. This *covering*, the robe of His own righteousness, Christ will put upon every repenting, believing soul. . . . The guests at the marriage feast were inspected by the king. Only those were accepted who had obeyed his requirements and put on the wedding garment. So it is with the guests at the gospel feast. All must pass the scrutiny of the great King, and only those are received who have put on the robe of Christ's righteousness" (*Christ's Object Lessons*, pp. 310-312; italics supplied).

The man without the wedding garment in Jesus' parable stands in the same position as the thief and the perjurer in Zechariah's vision. They all do not have the covering of Christ, the giver of the robe and their judge. Consequently they received, to His great disappointment, the judgment of condemnation instead of what He really wanted to give them, the judgment of vindication.

Many other individuals were not visited by the flying scroll. It was sent forth on a precise mission to "enter," "abide," and "consume" the evildoers, who also in their own lives invited sin to enter, abide, and consume them (Zech. 5:3, 4). They brought this tragic end upon themselves by becoming comfortable with sin, allowing it to make residence in their midst and becoming engrossed in it. Imagine how different their situation might have been if they had related to the Lord with a similar commitment as they related to sin, by allowing Him to enter their hearts, make His residence in their midst, and become consumed with His love and life.

The Vision of the Woman in the Ephah. In Zechariah's seventh vision (Zech. 5:5-11) God showed the prophet a woman in the ephah closed with lead. We notice three main terms used to describe the first part of this vision: (1) *ephah*, (2) *lead*, (3) *woman*.

The Hebrew ephah was a dry measure of about 5 to 6 gallons and was used to measure the volume of grain and other products in commerce. Amos used the term *ephah* in connection with dishonest trading, and this corresponds with the motif of stealing in the previous vision (Amos 8:5; Haggai 2:16). Some merchants tried to make the ephah smaller to deceive customers.

The "leaden cover" literally meant a round disk of lead that covered the mouth of the ephah that Zechariah saw. Lead is heavy and indicates that wickedness, symbolized by the woman, must not get out and escape from the ephah.

Here the woman symbolized the wickedness of back-slidden Israel, which was always seeking to manifest itself among them. The word for wickedness in the Hebrew is *rishah*, which belongs to judgment terminology and characterizes the one who is declared guilty before a court. (See Eze. 18:20.) Also the symbol of "woman" represented wickedness in Revelation 2:20 and 17:3-7. There John identified her as "Jezebel" and the "mother of harlots," pointing to the apostate condition of the church in the Dark Ages and up to the present time.

Of course, we must add that woman in the Bible can also mean something very positive—the symbol of God's faithful church, which is clothed with the sun and stands upon the moon (Rev. 12:1). She fled into the wilderness when persecuted for her faithfulness to God (verses 5, 6, 13-17). Moreover, a woman symbolized Christ's bride—His church—which will be prepared to meet Him when He comes (Rev. 21:2, 9). It seems that in the Bible woman as a symbol could represent the worst or the best possible traits.

A drastic action was taken in casting the woman back into the ephah and thrusting the lead disk over it (Zech. 5:8). That type of action signified that God takes sin seriously. He wants to rid His people of it individually and purge the whole land. As we have seen earlier, the individuals who appropriated Christ's righteousness and His Spirit in their lives were saved, but the ones who refused, rebelling against the divine offer, were cut off. Now, symbolically, God gathers all that accumulated wickedness into a container and seals it with a heavy disk of lead. Treating sin like an infectious plague, He makes certain that it does not slip out to pollute His people again.

Evil is not something to be played with. It is infectious and deadly. It needs to be disposed of decisively before it consumes an individual. It does not belong in the lives of God's people, and it should be taken back to Babylon (symbol of evil) to stay there where it belongs.

Even though evil was tightly sealed in the ephah, it was

not left there but taken up by two women with wind in their storklike wings (verse 9). They represented instrumentalities through whom God would execute His mission. The angel does not explain who they are. However, it is sufficient to know that they were used for the important purpose of removing wickedness far away from Israel to the land of Shinar (verse 11).

The act of carrying the ephah was public—"between the heaven and the earth"—just like the flying scroll. In the judgment of God nothing will be hidden, for the whole universe will witness His acts of judgment. The destination of the ephah was the land of Shinar, where it was going to be established—"build a house for it" (verse 11). Shinar was the first world power built by Nimrod (Gen. 10:8-10; 11:2), and it was the same as Babylon. The tower of Babel was built in Shinar (Gen. 11:2-9). The Scriptures have a great deal to say about Babylon. It was a symbol of a world power hostile to God and His people, and God will eventually destroy it. Its fall is predicted and described (Rev. 14:8; 18:1-24), and God's wrath is visited upon it (Rev. 16:19).

Wickedness is an intruder among God's people. It tries to settle in their lives, and unfortunately sometimes it succeeds. But wickedness should not abide in Israel, because wickedness belongs to Babylon, the center of evil where a "house is built" for it—signifying permanent residence there where evil feels right at home.

In Zechariah's eighth vision (Zech. 6:1-8), the Lord judges the nations around Israel, but He does that after judging His own people individually and corporately in the sixth and seventh visions (Zech. 5:1-11). It is interesting that God's people are judged and purged from sin prior to His judgment falling on the other nations. Peter sheds some light on this point when he writes, "For the time has come for judgment to begin with the household of God; and if it begins with us, what will be the end of those who do not obey the gospel of God?" (1 Peter 4:17).

Ellen White addresses the subject of the investigative judgment in the context of Joshua's experience in Zechariah

3 and in the messages of Daniel and Revelation. She devotes a whole chapter to the subject in the book *The Great Controversy*, depicting the Day of Atonement thus: "In the typical service only those who had come before God with confession and repentance, and whose sins, through the blood of the sin offering, were transferred to the sanctuary had a part in the service of the Day of Atonement. So in the great day of final atonement and investigative judgment the only cases considered are those of the professed people of God. The judgment of the wicked is a distinct and separate work, and takes place at a later period" (p. 480).

As we compare Zechariah 5:9-11 with Leviticus 16:20-22, we find a relationship between the act of placing all the sins of Israel on the head of the scapegoat and sending it away into the wilderness, and the sending away of the ephah full of wickedness to Babylon. The scapegoat (Azazel) and the ephah both leave the camp of Israel never to return—to be lost in the wilderness or to reside in Babylon.

Notice the following progressive events in reviewing the way in which God through Zechariah reached out to His people. Judgment must be understood in the context of all that God offered and tried to do to restore them:

1. God returns to them.
2. He calls them to return to Him.
3. He offers the gift of His righteousness.
4. He offers the gift of the Holy Spirit.
5. The judgment and Day of Atonement.
6. The "cutting off" of those refusing to appropriate the gift of Christ's righteousness.
7. The purging of sin and placing it in the ephah (Zech. 5) and on the scapegoat (Lev. 16) representing Satan (Rev. 20:1-3, 7-10) to be sent away to Babylon, to the wilderness, or to the lake of fire.

"As the priest, in removing the sins from the sanctuary, confessed them upon the head of the scapegoat, so Christ will place all these sins upon Satan, the originator and instigator of sin" (*ibid.*, p. 485). "We are now living in the great day of atonement. In the typical service, while the high priest was making the atonement for Israel, all were required to afflict their souls by repentance of sin and humiliation before the Lord, lest they be cut off from among the people. In like manner, all who would have their names retained in the book of life should *now*, in the few remaining days of their probation, afflict their souls before God by sorrow for sin and true repentance. There must be deep, faithful searching of heart. The light, frivolous spirit indulged by so many professed Christians must be put away" (*ibid.*, pp. 489, 490).

Christ who is ministering now as our high priest (Heb. 4:14, 15; 9:24, 25) longs to cover us with His righteousness and be at-one-ment with us. Are we—right now—searching our hearts and examining our ways? Do we know from the depths of our being that Christ has become the center of our lives? During this special time of probation, the Lord in His patience and love, "not wishing that any should perish, but that all should reach repentance" (2 Peter 3:9), is making His final plea to us before He comes. He wants to vindicate us and not condemn us, because "there is therefore now no condemnation for those who are in Christ Jesus" (Rom. 8:1). The crucial and urgent question is Are we "in Christ Jesus" now? Are we doing our best to walk in the Spirit more and more every day?

Peter admonishes us that since the coming of the Lord is upon us, "what sort of persons ought you to be in lives of holiness and godliness, waiting for and hastening the coming of the day of God" (2 Peter 3:11, 12). But are we eagerly awaiting His glorious appearing? Do our lives show that through Christ we are living godly and holy lives? He desires to come soon and take us unto Himself, but do we really want Him to come? Where do we stand now in our relationship with Christ?

Christ told the parable of the ten virgins, "illustrating the experience of the church that shall live just before His second coming" (*Christ's Object Lessons*, p. 406). The messenger to the remnant church gives relevant counsel relating to the day of atonement and the coming of Christ the

Bridegroom: "The ten virgins are watching in the evening of this earth's history. All claim to be Christians. . . . All are apparently waiting for Christ's appearing. But five are unready" (*ibid.*, pp. 412, 413).

But why were they unprepared? She lists some reasons. Do any of these same reasons exist in your life? "In this life they have not entered into fellowship with Christ; therefore they know not the language of heaven." "The class represented by the foolish virgins are not hypocrites . . . but they have not yielded themselves to the Spirit's working." They "have been content with a superficial work. They do not know God. They have not studied His character; they have not held communion with Him; therefore they do not know how to trust, how to look and live." "They have no oil in their vessels with their lamps. They are destitute of the Holy Spirit" (*ibid.*, pp. 413, 411, 408).

God forbid that any of us end up being foolish like those five virgins! Our eternal destiny does not have to end up in that tragic fashion at all. Today as we hear the voice of the Holy Spirit speak to us, let us not harden our hearts (Heb. 3:7, 8). May we give our Lord all of us and receive all of Him so that "our thoughts are with Him, and our sweetest thoughts are of Him. All we have and are is consecrated to Him. We long to bear His image, breathe His spirit, do His will, and please Him in all things" (*Steps to Christ*, p. 58). May holding sweet communion with Christ become an integral part of our daily lives so that we may learn to trust Him naturally in all things, and to look up to Him in all circumstances and live. May we never be destitute of the Holy Spirit, but like Jesus our example receive daily "a fresh baptism of the Holy Spirit" (*Christ's Object Lessons*, p. 139).

We need to have an intimate and abiding experience with Christ in order to live godly lives and be prepared to meet what is coming upon this world. As Christ prepares to conclude His high priestly ministry during this antitypical Day of Atonement, Satan knows that his time is short and that this will be his last chance to overcome God's remnant. So with great wrath and vengeance he attacks those who in

Christ valiantly resist him. That is why it is imperative that we abide in Christ, covered and protected in His perfect robe of righteousness. That is and will be our only confidence and safety.

"Zechariah's vision of Joshua and the Angel applies with *peculiar* force to the experience of God's people in the *closing* scenes of the great day of atonement. The *remnant church* will then be brought into great trial and distress. Those who *keep the commandments of God and the faith of Jesus* will feel the ire of the dragon and his hosts. Satan numbers the world as his subjects; he has gained control even of many professing Christians. But here is a *little company* who are resisting his supremacy. If he could blot them from the earth, his triumph would be complete" (*Prophets and Kings*, p. 587; italics supplied).

But thank God for Jesus and His righteousness. Satan will be completely vanquished, and the remnant church will triumph in Christ. The holy angels of God will be sealing Christ's own, who are so settled and rooted in Him that no one and no power will be able to separate them from His love. In *Prophets and Kings*, page 591, Ellen White quotes Zechariah 3:4 in relationship to the time when the remnant people of God are sealed. May this statement describe our own experience: "The despised remnant are clothed in glorious apparel, nevermore to be defiled by the corruptions of the world. Their names are retained in the Lamb's book of life. . . . Now they are eternally secure from the tempter's devises. . . . While Satan has been urging his accusations, holy angels, unseen, have been passing to and fro, placing upon the faithful ones the seal of the living God."

Christ
the Branch

The image of the Branch emerges as the heart of the book of Zechariah. It is the Branch who defends Joshua and covers him with His righteousness, and it is He who through His Spirit empowers Zerubbabel to rebuild the Temple. He is the force behind all God's activities of redemption and restoration.

In this chapter we will concentrate on those passages that touch on the subject of the Branch. Here is a sketch of these passages:

"My Servant the Branch"	"Behold the Man"
(Zech, 3:8-10)	(Zech. 6:9-15)
1. The Servant Branch	1. Joshua Crowned
2. The Stone	2. The Man Branch
3. His Functions	3. His Functions
(a) Removes the guilt	(a) Builds the Temple
(b) Vine and fig tree	(b) Bears the glory
	(c) Priest on throne
	(d) Counsel of peace
	4. Diligent Obedience

My Servant the Branch. In the vision of Joshua's cleansing and restoration as high priest, Christ is presented as the Servant Branch, the Saviour of His people, who will "remove the guilt of this land in a single day" (Zech. 3:8, 9). This Servant Branch totally obeys His Father and fully gives Himself to humanity. Isaiah depicts this righteous Servant

Branch as making many to be accounted righteous, bearing their iniquities, and making intercession for them (Isa. 53:11, 12). And the apostle Paul describes Christ as emptying "himself, taking the form of a servant" and becoming "obedient unto death, even death on a cross" (Phil. 2:7, 8).

The Old Testament contains at least four major references to the Messiah as the Branch. In these four Messianic references we find four portraits of the Christ:

1. The divine and righteous King comes from the seed of David as the heir of righteousness. He is called The Lord Our Righteousness and brings salvation (Jer. 23:5, 6; 33:15).

2. **The Servant Branch** accomplishes God's eternal purpose to save humanity (Zech. 3:8).

3. **The Man Branch** represents the human race in His incarnation as the Son of Man—the true Man (Zech. 6:12).

4. **The God Branch**, the Branch of Yahweh, is the Son of God (Isa. 4:2).

Zechariah 3:8, 9 refers to the Servant Branch as a single, engraved stone with seven eyes. It brings the promise that Israel's guilt will one day be removed. Just as the seven eyes of the Lord in Zechariah 4:10 point to His perfect knowledge and omnipresence, so also do the eyes of this unique stone. The removal of the guilt from the people corresponds to the removal of guilt from Joshua (Zech. 3:4). It also has its eschatological implication for the future. On the day of the Lord, when He returns, He will remove all guilt and sin from the whole earth by casting it on the head of Satan. We may compare this eschatological "stone" to that mentioned in Daniel 2:34, 35, 44, where the stone "cut out by no human hand" destroys all worldly kingdoms and establishes His own eternal kingdom.

Moreover, the "one day" can refer to the death of Jesus on the cross, when He took upon Himself the guilt and sin of the world so that whoever accepts Him may be covered with His righteousness. (See 1 Peter 3:18; Heb. 9:25-28.) In Revelation 5:6 John saw "a Lamb standing, as though it had been slain" (RSV), with seven horns and seven eyes. Here the seven eyes of Christ are associated with His crucifixion when He removed the guilt of the world by placing it upon Himself.

The engraving on the stone indicates something permanent; so also God's offer of forgiveness and peace is definite and sure for all who seek Him. He is the tested and firm foundation stone—a precious cornerstone who will not disappoint anyone who trusts in Him (Isa. 28:16). Certainly the imagery of a stone suitably describes Christ and is mentioned frequently in the Bible. He was the Rock who followed the children of Israel in the wilderness (1 Cor. 10:4), and He is the Rock on whom the church is built (Matt. 16:18).

Guilt is a terrible thing to experience, for it weighs heavily on the mind, and its burden crushes the spirit. No one can ever remove this burden of guilt except the Lord Jesus. He alone can take away our personal guilt. Imagine if there were no way to remove this guilt! How grateful we should always be for this unique and inestimable ministry of our Servant Branch.

Security, peace, and prosperity ensue when God removes His people's guilt. "In that day . . . every one of you will invite his neighbor under his vine and under his fig tree" (Zech. 3:10). Verse 10 is closely linked with verse 9 by the repetition of the word *day*. The "single day" (verse 9) in which He removes the guilt is the same as "that day" (verse 10).

The vines and the fig trees, native to Palestine, came to symbolize Israel. Planting, enjoying the fruits of the harvest, and resting unhurriedly with family and friends under the cool shade of these trees signified peace, joy, and prosperity. This is the natural result, isn't it, when the heavy burden of guilt and sin is lifted?

Behold the Man. The three men who arrived from Babylon gave Zechariah gifts of silver and gold, which he used to make a crown for Joshua. Immediately after he placed the crown on Joshua's head the Lord tells Joshua, "Behold, the man whose name is the Branch" (Zech. 6:11, 12). What, then, is the relationship between Joshua and the Man Branch? As in Zechariah 3:1-4 Joshua represented his sinful people, so here he serves as a type of King Messiah who will act on behalf of His people.

The Man Branch "shall grow up in his place, and he shall build the temple of the Lord" (Zech. 6:12). When we compare this text with Isaiah 11:1, which mentions the "Branch," and the "root out of a dry ground" in Isaiah 53:2, we see a close connection. These three references allude to plant growth by using words such as *root, stem, branch, plant,* and *shoot.* That is how God thought of His people. He had such great hopes for them! They were to be like a tree that would grow and spread its branches, but as a result of their rebellion, God had chastised His people by cutting down this tree, exiling them to Babylon. However, God in His mercy left a root and a stump (Isa. 11:1), symbol of hope and restoration that someday a tree—namely, the promised Messiah—would grow from the root of David.

The following sketch compares and contrasts the Branch with the stump as pictured in Isaiah 53:2; 11:1; 4:2; and Zechariah 6:12. What would your life be without the living Branch?

The Stump	The Branch
1. Same ground—dry	1. Same ground—dry
2. Same seed—David's	2. Same seed—David's
3. Dead stump	3. Living Branch
4. Evil stump	4. Righteous Branch
5. No hope	5. Hope
6. No fruit	6. Fruit

The "dry ground" symbolizes the dryness and barrenness of Israel's spiritual life. Out of hopelessness comes forth hope, and out of a dry stump springs forth a living Branch, a promise of a new beginning and a new life. This Living Branch would succeed where the dry stump, the Jewish nation, had failed.

The Living Branch is a promise of a new beginning for us today also. Do you feel that your life is like a dry stump in a dry ground? Let the seed of David, the Living Branch, grow in your life and give you hope, righteousness, and a spiritually fruitful life.

Zechariah 6:12, 13 shows this Man Branch as an active person, which is indicated by the several active verbs used to describe His work. Notice the following diagram of this passage:

What the Man Branch will do	Reference
1. "He shall **grow up** out of his place"	verse 12 (KJV)
2. "He shall **build** the temple of the Lord"	verse 12
3. "Even he shall **build** the temple of the Lord"	verse 13 (KJV)
4. "He shall **bear** the glory"	verse 13 (KJV)
5. He "shall **sit** and **rule** upon his throne"	verse 13
6. "He shall **be** a priest upon his throne"	verse 13 (KJV)

The repetition and emphasis placed on the pronoun "He," referring to the Branch, and reinforced by "Even He," affirms the definite and grand work that He will accomplish. Also this idea is strengthened by the frequent use of action verbs such as *grow up, build, bear the glory,* and *sit* and *rule.* The promise "He shall build the temple of the Lord" is repeated twice for emphasis.

We know that the Man Branch (working through Zerubbabel) was the real Builder of the Temple. But more important, He builds the temple of His presence in our midst. He calls His body a temple in Matthew 26:61. And in His incarnation He became the fulfillment of "He shall build the temple of the Lord" (Zech. 6:12) by becoming flesh and tabernacling among us. In Christ was revealed God's presence and glory: "He who has seen me has seen the Father" (John 14:9). Furthermore, in Christ humanity was reconciled to God. He in His person, the embodiment of God's power, presence, and glory (Col. 2:9), is the *meeting place*—the Temple—where God and His people hold communion and are reconciled.

Finally in this chapter we will consider the Man Branch

as the *King Priest* symbolized by Joshua. Even though he was the high priest, he was crowned as king to show that Christ combined in Himself the two divine offices that fulfilled the dual functions of king/priest. Zerubbabel and Joshua contributed to and were types of the work of the promised Branch. While they could not—either alone or together—adequately represent Christ's functions as king and priest, He combines perfectly and harmoniously the two offices in Himself.

As we examine how Zechariah 6:13 (KJV) illustrates the kingly and priestly functions combined in the Messiah, we notice the following literary pattern of A B A B AB:

1. "And he **shall build** . . ."	(kingly)	A
2. "And he **shall bear the glory**"	(priestly)	B
3. And He "shall **sit and rule** upon his **throne**"	(kingly)	A
4. "And he **shall be a priest** upon his **throne**"	(priestly)	B
5. "Counsel of peace **shall be between them**"	(kingly/priestly)	AB

The verse ends with the fitting summary of the kingly/priestly functions that the Man Branch would combine. Harmony, understanding, and peace shall be between such kingly/priestly functions combined in Christ the Branch.

Christ in His first advent became our high priest (Heb. 2:17), and in His second advent will come as our victorious king (Matt. 25:31). The Messiah Branch perfectly blends these two offices. (See Heb. 4:14; Rev. 19:16; and Jer. 23:5, 6.) He can also be compared to Melchizedek, who combined the two functions of king/priest (Heb. 5:5-10; 7:1, 2).

Harmony, counsel of peace—do we find these in working together as a church in building up the body of Christ? Pastors and administrators working harmoniously together for the Lord. Academics, evangelists, medical professionals, and others cooperating together in unity and peace to advance the kingdom of our King and Priest.

The Branch is not only the Branch of Israel, but also of the whole world, for "those who are far off" (Zech. 6:15). In

Christ the walls of separation among different peoples have been broken down, so that the ones who are near and the ones who are far off may meet as one in Christ (Eph. 2:13, 17). In a sense this is a missionary outreach to other nations beyond Israel. Indeed, God planned to have other nations learn about Him through the witness of His people, so that they too might join them in building His spiritual temple in their lives and experience His presence and blessings.

Tragically, literal Israel did not meet God's conditions in forming that spiritual house where all peoples might commune with the true God. He admonished them to obey Him diligently in order to have such promises fulfilled in their lives (Zech. 6:15). But God's purpose is being fulfilled today in the establishment of spiritual Israel from every nation.

Consider this question: Am I diligent in maintaining the vital connection between the living Branch and my dry stump? Seeking the Branch Christ to revitalize us and to build His residence in our lives is the most important task ever. Our eternal destiny depends on it. "We are not to walk with God for a time, and then part from His company and walk in the sparks of our own kindling. There must be a firm continuance, a perseverance in acts of faith. . . . No one of us will gain the victory without persevering, untiring effort, proportionate to the value of the object which we seek, even eternal life" (*Testimonies to Ministers*, p. 511).

For Christ's Sake

One day the new pastor of a district was visiting his parishioners to get acquainted and let them know he cared. In one of the homes, he visited with both parents and children, taking genuine interest in their comments and experiences. At the end of the visit he told them how much he enjoyed the opportunity of fellowshiping with each one of them. He then offered a prayer and prepared to leave. The mother gently interrupted him, saying that her family greatly appreciated his visit but asked if he had forgotten to tell them something. She wondered aloud if the church was having a fund drive, or if there was a particular problem he wished to discuss with them. The pastor, slightly puzzled, explained with all sincerity that there was, in fact, no program or problem to discuss and that the only reason he had come was for them—for their own sake. Moved by his honest response and with tears forming in her eyes, she said that others had come around to visit but often for some other reason. "This is the first time a pastor has come for nothing else except to get better acquainted with us," she said.

This chapter focuses on the profound exchange between the Lord and His people in terms of their ethical behavior and the real motives behind their service and religious practices. It seems that some Israelites had ulterior motives in serving God and their neighbors. Selfish reasons prompted them, and they did things for their own sake but not for the Lord's sake (Zech. 7:5, 6).

Christ's motive for relating to us is His love. "But God demonstrates His own love toward us, in that while we were still sinners, Christ died for us" (Rom. 5:8, NKJV). We definitely had nothing to recommend us to Christ, for we were even His enemies. He came for us, for our own sake, because of His great love. What prompts our religious practices and our service to God? Do we act for Christ's sake? Is our behavior toward Him and others motivated by Christ's love or by our own love for self? True religion moves beyond what people can see on the outside to what God sees on the inside.

This chapter will focus on Zechariah 7. We will explore the way in which the returned exiles practiced their fasting, what it told about their true motives, and how God exhorted them to examine their hearts and respond to His love. The Lord was concerned about His people's occupation with their own self-centered traditions, which did not lead to a genuine relationship with Him. Any religious act must be God-centered, not man-centered; otherwise such act in reality leads to self-worship.

A delegation from the town of Bethel trekked to Jerusalem to inquire about practices of fasting and mourning (Zech. 7:1-3). This delegation was apparently sent because such issues weighed heavily on their minds. In response to their inquiry, God raised three questions of His own—questions calculated to help them examine their true motives. And His response was not just directed to them, but also included "all the people of the land and the priests" (verse 5). What they needed most was not a superficial answer to some ritual practice, but a deep probing of their hearts by God to help them focus on Him and set their spiritual priorities straight. In His probing questions God reminded them that in pretending to fast, eat, and drink for Him they were actually fasting, eating, and drinking for themselves (verses 5, 6). He also reminded them of the counsels of the former prophets that they ignored, resulting in the calamities they mourned and fasted for (verse 7).

They overlooked the crucial fact that He wanted them to

hear and obey His words, directing their attention to Him, not to themselves and their obsession with their misfortunes. One way of looking at their eating and drinking for themselves (verse 6) is to compare that with hearing the words of the Lord in the subsequent verse (verse 7). True fasting and true eating in a spiritual sense means fasting from men's words and feasting on God's words. Spiritually we become what we eat. If we eat God's words, we become more like Him; and if we feed on our own words, we become more self-centered. God wants us to stop rehearsing in our minds our disappointments and discouragements, and to start trusting Him and what He wants to do for us. "It is a positive duty to resist melancholy, discontented thoughts and feelings—as much a duty as it is to pray" (*The Ministry of Healing*, p. 251). "All the fasting in the world will not take the place of simple trust in the word of God" (*Counsels on Diet and Foods*, p. 189).

The Israelites showed their selfishness and wrong motivation not only in their relationship with God, but also in their mistreatment of others around them. It is true that if we serve God from the wrong motives, we also relate to others from wrong motives, too. In God's exhortation to them (verses 8-10) we find first two do's and then two don'ts: Do render true judgments, and do show kindness and mercy. Then do not oppress the widow, the fatherless, the sojourner, or the poor; and do not devise evil in your heart. God does not only say what they should not do, but also what they should do. Moreover, He begins His exhortation with the positive do's before He mentions the don'ts. It is neither enough nor productive to tell people what is wrong. We must also know what is right—a way out. We need positive things to do to replace the negative things we did before. Our God is the kind of person who not only tells us what the problem is, but He also shows us the solution to meet that particular problem.

What does it mean to render *true* judgment? It has to do with treating others fairly and honestly—and with clean motives. Haven't you found it refreshing to deal with someone who is always fair and not partial or a respecter of persons? We all appreciate these much-needed qualities. We can see in these exhortations from God the spirit of the Sermon on the Mount. God goes beyond the letter of the law right to the heart and the spirit of the law. Both the Zechariah and Matthew references go beyond the surface and probe deeply into the real motives and intentions. This is the level that God looks at: "For the Lord does not see as man sees; for man looks at the outward appearance, but the Lord looks at the heart" (1 Sam. 16:7, NKJV). Not oppressing the widow, the fatherless, the stranger, or the poor and not imagining evil in one's heart against one's neighbor form the crux of heart religion. It is totally different from the religion of appearance, which encourages the outward show of mourning and fasting. To be kind to strangers and widows goes beyond the limits of legal duty. The way we relate to such people reveals our true motives and uncovers what we are really like on the inside.

"He [the Christian] lives constantly as in the presence of God, knowing that every thought is open to the eyes of Him with whom we have to do. . . . They [Christ's words] condemn the deceptive compliments, the evasion of truth, the flattering phrases, the exaggerations. . . . They teach that no one who tries to appear what he is not, or whose words do not convey the real sentiment of his heart, can be called truthful" (*Thoughts From the Mount of Blessing*, pp. 67, 68).

It is disappointing that God's loving exhortation of His people went unheeded. In mentioning three actions that are associated with three parts of the human body, Zechariah describes vividly how they turned away from Him. In the following sketch of Zechariah 7:11, 12 notice their gradual and progressive rejection of God:

Body Part	**Action**	**Reference**
1. Shoulder	Pulled it away	verse 11, KJV
2. Ears	Stopped them	verse 11

| 3. Heart | Made it like adamant | verse 12 |

Zechariah's phraseology leads progressively to a climax. First, the people did not hearken and cooperate with God, showing a very negative attitude. They did not want God to search their hearts and know their ways, thus spurning a clean heart and a right spirit (Ps. 51:10). Second, they pulled away the shoulder—like an ox that stubbornly pulls away from the yoke to be placed upon its shoulders. Not hearkening to God's voice leads to stubbornness and to disrespect for God's message, which in turn leads to closing the ears to the voice of God and quenching the opportunities of being influenced by His Spirit. Then with time the heart becomes hardened like a stone. The word *adamant* is translated from the Hebrew word *shamir*, which refers to a stone of exceeding hardness.

The people deliberately chose to ignore God, and His strongest appeals could not soften and penetrate their *shamir* hearts. Progressively they separated themselves from Him. And here He is, with a compassionate and loving heart, reminding the returned exiles of the reasons that calamities had befallen them and their parents. He is pleading with them to learn valuable lessons from such experiences and to turn their hearts to Him. The only solution to their hearts of hard stone is for them to accept and appropriate His promise in Ezekiel 11:19, "And I will give them one heart, and put a new spirit within them; I will take the stony heart out of their flesh and give them a heart of flesh."

We must, of course, apply what we have studied about the experiences of God's people to our lives today. Let us ponder prayerfully our own motives, ethical standards, and behavior. What difference would it make in the quality of our Christian lives and witness if we did all things as if we were doing them unto the Lord? And that is the only true motive for whatever we do in this life. For He said, "Truly, I say unto you, as you did it to one of the least of these my brethren, you did it to me" (Matt. 25:40).

Christ the Hope
of the Remnant

No other example speaks more eloquently of the remnant than does the mighty defense the Lord leveled against Satan in behalf of Joshua and the returned exiles of Judah: "Is not this a brand plucked from the fire?" (Zech. 3:2). Imagine picking a twig from a burning heap of dry branches. You risk the raging fire, snatching it swiftly in your hand. This twig—almost consumed and still spewing fire and smoke—is rescued just in the nick of time. Zechariah uses this powerful image to portray how Christ saves the remnant of His people, risking all—even His own life—in order to rescue and preserve them from certain destruction. He holds them close to His heart, and no power can tear them away from his grasp. They are "the apple of his eye" (Zech. 2:8, KJV) and "the jewels of a crown" (Zech. 9:16).

Christ ransomed us not with silver or gold but with His own precious blood (1 Peter 1:19). He invested His life in us and He values us as much, if not more, than He values Himself. We live by hope in Him, and He does everything in His power to keep that hope alive. To those who seem hopeless to others, He holds a promise of hope. "A bruised reed he will not break, and a smoldering wick he will not snuff out" (Isa. 42:3, NIV). The "Branch" is the only hope for the "brand." The Messiah Branch is alive and strong, and He will give His life to all the endangered "brands" who submit to Him.

Chapter 8 of Zechariah places a lot of emphasis on the theme of the remnant. Several times Zechariah alludes to the remnant in that chapter, which is saturated with the Lord's own words and promises. These promises comprise 10 messages of encouragement and hope, each introduced by the format "thus says the Lord of hosts." Four times they include "let your hands be strong" and "fear not." This repetition and emphasis reveals clearly the certainty, hope, and trustworthiness of His promises. Here in this chapter we find an upbeat and hopeful portrayal of what Jerusalem will be if His people obey Him. So concerned that His people be restored to Him, God portrays an optimistic picture of what will come to pass if they obey. He hopes that such promises of the great blessings awaiting them will inspire them to follow Him with all their hearts.

He inspires such hope by promising that He will return to Israel and dwell among them. Consequently, "Jerusalem shall be called the faithful city, and the mountain of the Lord of hosts, the holy mountain" (Zech. 8:3). This verse speaks of a city and a mountain, which are connected with two important adjectives: *faithful* and *holy*. The "holy mountain" refers to Jerusalem (Isa. 27:13; 66:20). Therefore the promised Jerusalem will be distinguished by two important virtues: truthfulness and holiness. In this verse the word for truth in Hebrew is *'emeth*, which means "stability," "trustworthiness," and "faithfulness," hence the "faithful city."

Jerusalem, the kind of city God had in mind, would live up to its name. Its inhabitants—the remnant—would live the meaning of the name. They would be faithful and holy, because God who dwells among them is faithful and holy. This prophecy will perfectly and ultimately be fulfilled in the New Jerusalem with the remnant of spiritual Israel.

Zechariah 8:4, 5 depicts a beautiful picture of Jerusalem's streets, where old men and women, boys and girls, freely move about in perfect peace and security. The old and the young are usually the most vulnerable against danger, famine, and war; and the very fact that they live in such tranquillity and safety proves that the ideal circumstances exist in Jerusalem.

How is a city evaluated? By its tall buildings, wealth,

technology? No, not really. It is evaluated by how it treats the two groups most overlooked—the old and the young. In this materialistic and fast-moving society, often it is not difficult to ignore the very young as well as the elderly. People are too often valued for what they can produce financially, and the young and those old in years are usually nonproductive. The young are not employed, and the old are retired. Especially the retired, no matter how influential they were before, are often ignored even by their own family members. What about the streets of a city? To a great degree they tell us about the quality of its life. Are the streets safe at night or even during the daytime for children and the elderly to move about freely without being assaulted? How tragically short of the ideal some of our cities fall, with all the murder, assault, and rape that take place daily.

The Lord asks a question of His people that initially seems somewhat puzzling, but on closer examination it reveals how much He wants to do to accomplish what looks like the impossible. "If it is marvelous in the sight of the remnant of this people in these days, should it also be marvelous in my sight, says the Lord of hosts?" (Zech. 8:6). The word *marvelous* comes from the Hebrew term *pala'*, which may have two meanings: to be too difficult and to be conspicuous or different. Combining these two meanings together, we may infer that Israel's lack of faith, in a sense, made it impossible for God to do what He would otherwise have done if they had trusted Him. Nothing is too difficult for the Lord, for He will effectuate such marvelous things as He has never done before.

So verse 6 is not necessarily a question. It is possibly a statement of irony, which, for emphasis' sake, could mean that this marvelous thing is going to be even a wonder to God. God plans to excel Himself, so to speak (if that is even possible). Ephesians 3:20 fits very well in this context. "Now to him who by the power at work within us is able to do far more abundantly than all that we ask or think."

Repeatedly God expresses His yearning to dwell among them so that He might be their God and they might be His people (Zech. 8:8). He wants His relationship with them to be reciprocal, based on mutual love, respect, and faithfulness. He always keeps His part of the covenant, and to motivate His people to be faithful to their part, He paints a picture in Zechariah 8:9-13 of the great blessings He will shower upon them. In verse 11 we find a transition line between what His rebellious people experienced in the past, and how He will deal with the remnant who returned from Babylon. This message of hope for the remnant begins and ends with words that encourage them to be strong and not afraid.

Perhaps a chart can make these verses more clear:

1. **Introduction**: "Let your hands be strong" verse 9

2. Poverty. Scarcity of materials, food, money verse 10

3. External opposition—hostile neighbors verse 10

4. Internal dissension among themselves verse 10

5. **The turning point**: God will deal differently with the **remnant** than in the former days verse 11

6. The **remnant** will possess all things verse 12

7. The **remnant** will be a blessing and not a curse verse 13

8. **Conclusion**: The **remnant** to fear not and be strong verse 13

Next God calls His remnant to sanctification and social righteousness (verses 14-19), mentioning two things as a preface: (1) He "purposed in these days to do good to Jerusalem," and He lifts up their spirits with (2) "fear not" (verse 15). He then proceeds to exhort them to righteousness. Only as God remains active in the life, infusing faith, courage, and hope, can one fulfill His moral and ethical imperatives. He longs to unite us to Himself and work in us according to His good pleasure.

These moral and ethical expectations of the remnant are: (1) speaking the truth, (2) rendering true judgment, (3) not imagining evil, and (4) not making false oaths. Then this passage directly mentions or implies several important spiritual virtues. Such virtues must be the basis for any and all conduct. They are (1) love, (2) truth, (3) peace, (4) joy, (5) honesty, and (6) purity. These qualifications for the remnant who were preparing for Christ's first advent are compatible with and summed up by the identifying marks of the remnant church in these last days, who are preparing for the Second Advent. "Here is the patience of the saints; here are those who keep the commandments of God and the faith of Jesus" (Rev. 14:12, NKJV).

Joy and gladness in the Lord are an honest expression that He indeed resides in the heart. In Zechariah 8:19 God comes across as a God of joy in changing their fasts of mourning into feasts of rejoicing. He desires His remnant to contemplate His mercy and love and not to dwell on their past gloomy events. After all, He was with them, and the Temple and Jerusalem would soon be completely rebuilt. Why despair when there was great hope? Why commemorate destruction of the Temple while it was being rebuilt? If they will love truth and peace, and if they will occupy themselves with what is fair and righteous, then that will take care of the sad memories and transform them into happy occasions.

The triangle of the three virtues of truth, justice, and peace is the bedrock on which the moral world is founded —and in that order. We must always start with the truth, which implies not only knowing truth but being truthful. Truth leads to justice, and where there is justice there is peace. Then just as we hate falsehood and evil, we must also love and pursue truth and peace. Love constitutes the only and greatest motivation for being truthful and being peace-makers. And in lovingly practicing truth, justice, and peace, we experience joy and gladness.

The remnant of God is a witnessing remnant as we look at the last verse of chapter 8. It is one of the most powerful statements about evangelism. "Let us go with you, for we have heard that God is with you" (verse 23). The remnant of the returned exiles were to lead the nations around them to a true knowledge of God. Their greatest drawing power would be not in themselves as such, but in the fact that God was with them. That is the most powerful and the only way to draw others to God.

As a result of this great evangelistic endeavor, a universal remnant would join the remnant of Israel. (See Zech. 8:20-23; 9:7; 14:16.) For example, even their enemies the Philistines were to be given the opportunity to turn to the true God. God is talking not of their destruction but of their salvation (Zech. 9:7). However, the remnant of Israel failed to accomplish that great task of preparing the world for Christ's first advent.

But we are the spiritual remnant of these last days, and God has entrusted us with the task of preparing a universal remnant that will meet Christ when He comes the second time. God forbid that we will fail as they failed. With Christ the hope of the remnant working through us, we will accomplish the task of readying a universal remnant to march to the New Jerusalem.

Christ Our Saviour and King

The book of Zechariah in its predominant theme of the Messiah takes into consideration His first, second, and third advents. In this chapter we will concentrate on Christ's first and second comings as sketched in chapter 9 of Zechariah. The third coming will be addressed in the last chapter of this book. In Zechariah Christ is the Lord of the "coming," and how pertinent this truth is today to the Advent movement and to all "who love his appearing" (2 Tim. 4:8, KJV).

In the very heart of chapter 9, amid war and destruction, we gleam a radiant image of the meekness, peace, justice, and triumph of the coming Messiah. Verse 9 portrays Him as the humble king who brings redemption from sin. And immediately following in verse 10 we catch a glimpse of His second advent in power and glory when He will bring eternal peace and establish His righteous sovereignty over the whole earth. These two verses, which fall in the center of the chapter, are interjected between verses 1-8 and verses 11-17 and present what Christ will do in defending and restoring His people, thereby establishing His spiritual kingdom and His kingdom of glory. "And he shall command peace to the nations; his dominion shall be from sea to sea" (verse 10).

Ellen G. White sheds some light on this Messianic prophecy of Christ's advents in *The Desire of Ages*. She writes, "Christ was following the Jewish custom for a royal entry. The animal on which He rode was that ridden by the kings of Israel, and prophecy had foretold that thus the

Messiah should come to His kingdom" (p. 570). "The triumphal ride of Christ into Jerusalem was the dim foreshadowing of His coming in the clouds of heaven with power and glory" (*ibid.*, p. 580).

Verses 2 through 7 of chapter 9 show how the Lord will defend His people by pulling down the wicked nations just prior to the First Coming. But also they show that out of the ruins of these nations He will bring forth a remnant for Himself. This remnant will join the remnant of Israel in preparation for the Saviour of mankind. God's undoing of these nations will embrace three things: He will destroy their wisdom, He will destroy their riches, and He will destroy their power (Zech. 9:2-4). Instead of pointing them to the true God, whatever these nations, such as Tyre and Sidon, acquired of earthly wisdom, riches, and power became a god to them. Consequently, they will experience three negative outcomes: Fear because they will perish, sorrow because they will be desolate, and shame because their pride will be cut off (verses 5-7).

However, the true wisdom, riches, and power were brought by Christ in His first coming to save mankind. The apostle Paul declares, "We preach . . . Christ the power of God and the wisdom of God. For the foolishness of God is wiser than men, and the weakness of God is stronger than men" (1 Cor. 1:24, 25). (See also 1 Cor. 1:18-20; 3:18-20.)

Earthly wisdom, riches, and power do not save any person or society. Tyre was clever, rich, and powerful in worldly and commercial affairs, but without God it was brought to nothing. But all the riches of heaven were given through Christ, and as Paul testified: "Indeed I also count all things loss for the excellence of the knowledge of Christ Jesus . . . for whom I have suffered the loss of all things, and count them as rubbish, that I may gain Christ" (Phil. 3:8, NKJV).

The Jewish nation and the other nations were not prepared for Christ's first coming because they depended too much on their own wisdom, resources, and power. Let us not repeat their failures as we prepare for Christ's second coming. We must not put our trust in our wisdom and resources, but we must "gain Christ" and depend more on His wisdom and resources to prepare us and others to meet Him when He comes again.

Now we come to the very heart of this chapter, the coming of the long-awaited Messiah. Zechariah 9:9 describes Christ's first advent, during which He entered Jerusalem. This important prophecy begins with the announcement of great joy and celebration because of the good news of His coming. Then it portrays the Messiah's character and what He will do. He is the Desire of Ages and the greatest event ever in the history of the world.

What kind of person will the coming King be? Zechariah clearly answers this question as seen in the following outline. (See also Matt. 21:5; John 12:15; Isa. 42:1-3.)

1. His coming is a source of great rejoicing and good news.

2. He comes as our king—He takes the initiative.

3. He is just and triumphant, bringing salvation.

4. He is meek—He comes riding on an ass bringing peace.

Meekness is not a virtue that most people in our society admire. It is often associated with weakness and cowardice. But Christ voluntarily emptied Himself, and from a position of strength in His Father, He became lowly in heart. The ass is often a source of ridicule. Used by farmers in their toil, it represents lowliness and peace.

The following outline, contrasting Him with a warrior king, can help us better appreciate the character of the King of Peace:

The King of Peace	A Warrior King
1. Lowly and meek	1. Proud and arrogant
2. An ass, a beast of labor	2. A war-horse, chariots
3. Entourage: children, peasants	3. Entourage: warriors
4. Trophies: captives of His love	4. Trophies: his enemies
5. Palm branches	5. Spears and swords

6. He comes to save	6. He comes to destroy
7. He comes to bring peace	7. He comes to bring war
8. Divine spiritual power	8. Human physical force
9. Spiritual kingdom	9. Earthly kingdom
10. Eternal	10. Temporal

Matthew 11:29 and Philippians 2:5-8 movingly portray Christ the Prince of Peace as meek and lowly in heart, and as having emptied Himself and become a servant. We can contrast these qualities with those of Satan and his followers by studying this pertinent statement. "Lucifer desired God's *power*, but not His *character*. He sought for himself the highest place, and every being who is actuated by his spirit will do the same. . . . Dominance becomes the prize of the strongest. The kingdom of Satan is a kingdom of force; every individual regards every other as an *obstacle* in the way of his own advancement, or a *steppingstone* on which he himself may climb to a higher place" (*The Desire of Ages*, pp. 435, 436; italics supplied).

The prophecy we are considering with respect to the First Advent (Zech. 9:9) was literally and precisely fulfilled in the New Testament. In fact, all the Gospel writers refer to its fulfillment in the life of Jesus. (See Matt. 21:1-11; Mark 11:1-11; Luke 19:29-44; John 12:12-15.) Even as early as the times of Genesis, there was an allusion to the coming of the Messiah described in Zechariah 9:9. The dying words of Jacob predict the continuation of Judah as the leader among the children of Israel until the coming of Shiloh, who is the promised Messiah, who will be "binding his foal unto the vine, and his ass's colt unto the choice vine" (Gen. 49:11, KJV). "This was Shiloh, the peace giver. It was He who declared Himself to Moses as the I Am. . . . He was the Desire of all nations, the Root and the Offspring of David" (*ibid.*, p. 52).

After Jesus' triumphal entry into Jerusalem He wept over her and told the priests and Pharisees: "For I tell you, you will not see me again, until you say, 'Blessed is he who comes in the name of the Lord' " (Matt. 23:39). Jesus is here clearly associating their rejection of Him at His first coming with His second coming. Such a link between these two comings is alluded to in Zechariah 12:10: when Christ shall come in His glory, the ones who pierced Him (First Coming) shall see Him and "mourn for him, as one mourns for an only child" (Second Coming). It also seems evident from the context and the language used in Matthew 24:30 and Revelation 1:7 that there is a connection between these two verses and Zechariah 12:10 and Zechariah 9:9. The revelator writes: "Behold, he is coming with the clouds, and every eye will see him, every one who pierced him" (Rev. 1:7).

Ellen G. White makes this link between the triumphal entry as foretold in Zechariah 9:9 and the mourning for Christ at His second coming by those who pierced Him (Zech. 12:10). "The triumphal ride of Christ into Jerusalem was the dim foreshadowing of His coming in the clouds of heaven with power and glory. . . . In prophetic vision Zechariah was shown that day of final triumph; and he beheld also the doom of those who at the First Advent had rejected Christ: 'They shall look upon me whom they have pierced, and they shall mourn for him' (Zech. 12:10)" (*ibid.*, p. 580).

The internal evidence of Zechariah 9:10 and 16 also alludes to Christ's second advent, because it shows that He will destroy the instruments of war, will establish His universal dominion "from sea to sea, and from the River to the ends of the earth," and He will reward His faithful remnant as jewels of a crown. All of this can only transpire when Christ comes again in His glory. We still have instruments of war, even greater than ever. Christ's universal kingdom of glory "from sea to sea" has not been established yet, and His final rewards of the saints have not yet been given. Also in verses 14-17 the language used is Second Coming language, such as "The Lord God will sound the trumpet" and "On that day the Lord their God will save them."

It is interesting to see the contrast between the "waterless pit" (verse 11) and the "stronghold" (verse 12). The waterless pit is dry, low, and dark just like a prison; but our stronghold is the Lord Himself. Do trying circumstances keep enclosing you in these dark pits and hindering you from fleeing to Christ our stronghold? "The blood of my covenant" (verse 11), He pledges, will set you free from the waterless pit. Christ fully understands all the difficulties and discouragements that you confront. Through the precious blood of His covenant shed on the cross at His first advent, you can submit yourself to Him, and He will save you when He comes again. He "will restore to you double" (verse 12). When Christ comes, the joys of heaven will more than compensate for all the sufferings of this world, and the most painful ordeals will fade into insignificance.

We often focus on *our* reward when Christ comes, but what about *His* reward? We who are covered with and are walking in Christ's righteousness, will be "the reward of all His sufferings, His humiliation, and His love" (*Thoughts From the Mount of Blessing*, p. 89). Why not give our Saviour and our coming King this reward by giving yourself to Him completely so you can live with Him for eternity? "Hearts that have been the battleground of the conflict with Satan, and that have been rescued by the power of love, are more precious to the Redeemer than are those who have never fallen. . . . He collected all the riches of the universe, and laid them down in order to buy the pearl. And Jesus having found it, resets it in His own diadem. 'For they shall be as the stones of a crown, lifted up as an ensign upon his land.' Zech. 9:16. 'They shall be mine, saith the Lord of hosts, in that day when I make up my jewels.' Mal. 3:17" (*Christ's Object Lessons*, p. 118).

Christi
Our Good Shepherd

My childhood experience of having a lamb for a pet made an indelible impression on my mind. I have fond memories of this lamb following me, on his own initiative, whenever or wherever I moved around our farm. I quickly became attached to him because he seemed so innocent, trusting, patient, and totally harmless. And when we think of Christ as "the Lamb of God, who takes away the sin of the world" (John 1:29), we begin to comprehend why the lamb appropriately symbolized Jesus our sacrifice and sin-bearer.

So why, then, are we considering the Lamb if our subject at hand is the Good Shepherd? Because Zechariah 10 and 11 present such a vast difference between the Good Shepherd and false, murderous shepherds. He is so committed to His sheep in every way that He who is Himself the shepherd also becomes a lamb. He became one of them—us, takes excellent care of them—us, and He even gives His life for them—us. On the other hand, the false shepherds not only do not care for the sheep, but they harass and scatter them—even killing and feeding on them. Thank God for the Lamb/Good Shepherd, who gave His life for us and who constantly restores our souls and leads us in His paths of righteousness (Ps. 23:1-3).

In this chapter we will see a portrait of the Messiah as the Good Shepherd depicted in Zechariah 10. Then in Zechariah 11 we will see the tragic consequences of Israel's rejection of their Good Shepherd by submitting themselves to evil shepherds. In these two chapters the term *shepherd* is mentioned close to 14 times, and the term *flock* or *sheep* is alluded to at least eight times. These two chapters contain so many references to shepherding that we conclude this is their main theme.

The Good Shepherd knows that the people are "afflicted for want of a shepherd," for they were wandering like scattered sheep (Zech. 10:2). And because He "cares for his flock" (verse 3), He goes about providing them with pastures and abundant showers of rain to keep the grass green and plentiful (verse 1). This brings to mind Matthew 9:36, "When he saw the crowds, he had compassion for them, because they were harassed and helpless, like sheep without a shepherd."

The "latter rain" mentioned in Zechariah 10:1 (KJV) would come in the spring at the end of the rainy season to help mature the crop for the harvest. This rain also has a spiritual application, for it not only symbolizes the Lord's physical blessings, but more important, it represents the outpouring of His Spirit upon His people in the last days. (See Joel 2:23; Jer. 5:24.) The early rain would come in early fall, and it symbolized the outpouring of the Holy Spirit on the disciples at Pentecost.

So the first blessings that the Good Shepherd brings to His harassed people are the abundant showers to replace the drought. He sees to it that green vegetation replaces the parched desert. He presents His people with great incentives and prospects for following Him and shunning the false leaders who give them "empty consolation" (Zech. 10:2). In His great love He simply wants to enhance every possibility for them to trust Him and become His flock. The first such prospect He gives them is to "make them like his proud steed in battle" (verse 3). Although they appear as feeble, wandering sheep, He will transform them into strong instruments of victory—like a proven horse in battle. What transformation! From timid, lost, and helpless sheep to strong and courageous horses in God's battles.

Not only does God want to transform them into His mighty horse in battle, but He also gives them the greatest promise ever: The Messiah would come from them. Here He is represented by four symbols (verse 4): The Cornerstone, the Tent Peg, the Battle Bow, and every Ruler—all figurative terms associated with the Messiah. Indeed He did come from the tribe of Judah when He was born in Bethlehem.

Moreover, the Good Shepherd will give His people many other blessings as a result of being with them (see Zech. 10:5-8, 11-12): (1) They shall be strong, (2) they shall be saved, (3) He will have compassion on them, (4) they shall be as though not cast off, (5) He will answer them, (6) they shall rejoice, (7) He will whistle for them, (8) they shall be redeemed, (9) their enemies shall be defeated, and (10) they shall be strong in the Lord.

The assurance that the Lord will "have compassion on them" (verse 6) was fulfilled in the life of Christ. Many references in the Gospels show clearly that He was full of sympathy and compassion. (See Matt. 9:36; Mark 6:34; Luke 7:13.)

We are fortunate, indeed, as Christians to have such a compassionate Saviour! The gods of many heathen religions are cold, abstract, and unfeeling. But Christ has a heart that pulsates with compassion, love, and understanding toward us. "He who took humanity upon Himself knows how to sympathize with the sufferings of humanity. Not only does Christ know every soul, and the peculiar needs and trials of that soul, but He knows all the circumstances that chafe and perplex the spirit" (*The Ministry of Healing*, p. 249).

His compassion leads Him to treat His people "as though I had not rejected them" (Zech. 10:6). The Lord is a God of great incentives, which He uses to draw the wandering sheep back to Him. He appeals to His people to project themselves into the future to glimpse what a blessed relationship they will have with Him if they respond to His voice. In His great love He seems to search for ways to woo them back to Him. And despite all that they have done, He is willing to turn to a new page as though that is the very beginning of their relationship with Him.

When Jesus went out searching for the lost sheep, His

only concern was to find it, hold it close to His heart, and rejoice in bringing it back to the fold. "If you give yourself to Him, and accept Him as your Saviour, then, sinful as your life may have been, for His sake you are accounted righteous. Christ's character stands in place of your character, and you are accepted before God *just as if you had not sinned*" (*Steps to Christ*, p. 62; italics supplied).

How can "as though I had not rejected them" be experienced in our relationships with others? Are we prone to remember the bad as well as the good things about others? When we give ourselves to our perfect Lord, He remembers the good about us and forgets the bad. With His help we can treat others who have wronged us in the same way. "If we keep uppermost in our minds the unkind and unjust acts of others, we shall find it impossible to love them as Christ has loved us; but if our thoughts dwell upon the wondrous love and pity of Christ for us, the same spirit will flow out to others" (*ibid.*, p. 121).

In Zechariah 10:8, the Good Shepherd hisses or whistles to His flock. This is an interesting expression to describe the Lord. This word *hiss* in the KJV comes from the Hebrew *sharaq* and is employed in Isaiah 5:26 and 7:18, where we see a picture of God hissing to a nation, to a fly, and to a bee. In the context of Zechariah 10:8, the Good Shepherd is calling His scattered and lost people with a whistling sound, gathering them to Him just as the shepherd whistles to call his sheep to him. Hissing may indicate not only God calling His people but also His soothing, comforting, and reassuring ways. Our Good Shepherd does not hesitate to compare Himself to a hissing, whistling shepherd in order to reassure us of His loving presence.

In chapter 10 the Good Shepherd has done His utmost to attract His sheep to Him, but unfortunately in chapter 11 we see their rejection of their only hope and their submission to the evil shepherds committed to slaughter them. Were all His loving promises uttered to them in vain? Here in chapter 11 we see Israel oppressed by the evil shepherds instead of tended by the Good Shepherd, and the results are drastically different! Ezekiel joins Zechariah in giving a résumé of the Good Shepherd (Eze. 34:11-16; Zech. 10), and a résumé of the evil shepherds (Eze. 34:1-10; Zech. 11:16).

The Evil Shepherds	**The Good Shepherd**
1. Do not care for the perishing.	1. Rescues the perishing.
2. Ignore the wandering and lost.	2. Searches for the lost.
3. Do not treat the maimed, sick.	3. Heals the sick.
4. Do not nourish the sheep.	4. Feeds the sheep.
5. Do not strengthen the weak.	5. Strengthens the weak.
6. They are harsh. They howl.	6. He is gentle. He hisses.
7. They are absentee shepherds.	7. He is always among them.
8. They feed on the sheep.	8. He dies for the sheep.

The evil shepherds do not even take care of the healthy sheep, but the Good Shepherd cares for even the weakest sheep doomed for slaughter (Zech. 11:5, 7). He wants the unwanted, seeks the forsaken, and reaches out to the hopeless. The evil shepherds reveal their depraved spirit when they shamelessly assert, "Blessed be the Lord, I have become rich" (verse 5). They traffic in selling the sheep for the slaughter, and then brazenly claim that God is blessing their evil actions! It seems that their consciences are seared, and they do not feel any guilt. It is blasphemous when they give credit to God for that which He cannot condone or bless. There are people today like these evil shepherds who attribute certain actions to God, actions that He has nothing to do with. They are taking the Lord's name in vain.

God's long-suffering and patience is amazing, but His shattering of the two staffs called Grace and Union (verses 10, 14) denotes the withdrawal of His protection, defense, and patience. However, the breaking of the two staffs does not occur at the same time. The breaking of the staff known as Union takes place after the betrayal of Jesus for 30 shekels of silver (verses 12, 13). It signified Christ's rejection by the Jewish nation and His rejection of them. "The last appeal to Jerusalem had been in vain" and "In every age there is given to men their day of light and privilege, a probationary time in which they may become reconciled to God. But there is a limit to this grace. . . . That day had come to Jerusalem. Jesus wept in anguish over the doomed city, but He could not deliver her. He had exhausted every resource" (*The Desire of Ages*, pp. 580, 587).

But even though the Jewish nation rejected the Good Shepherd, a remnant of faithful Jews did not. The "poor of the flock," the small, faithful remnant to whom Jesus became the Shepherd (verses 4, 7, KJV), comes across as a breath of fresh air, so to speak, in the middle of rebellion, rejection, and broken covenants. Throughout the ages, no matter how gloomy the situation, a faithful remnant has always remained true to God.

We cannot help being utterly amazed at how patiently and lovingly Christ attempts to shepherd His ungrateful and rebellious flock. He exhausts all the means at His disposal to restore His people. He even gives His own life for them. What more could He have done? What about us who claim to be followers of Christ? Are we rejecting Him in our daily lives by giving allegiance to "false shepherds" or whatever takes the place of the Good Shepherd? Or are we "the poor of the flock," who follow Christ as their Good Shepherd? May it be said of us that we are "these who follow the Lamb wherever he goes" (Rev. 14:4).

Christit
the Lamb Slain

The Good Shepherd of chapters 10 and 11 becomes "the Lamb slain from the foundation of the world" (Rev. 13:8, KJV) and "the Lamb of God, who takes away the sin of the world" (John 1:29) in chapters 12 and 13. The Lamb suffers greatly for the wayward sheep, giving His life for them and thereby opening a fountain filled with blood. In the previous chapter we contrasted the Good Shepherd with the evil shepherds, who disdain, abuse, and kill the sheep. But the Good Shepherd cares so much for the sheep that He becomes the Lamb who, instead of taking their lives away, gives His own life for them.

The plan of salvation through Christ's shed blood was conceived before God created the world. The divine covenant, which assured that the Son of God would give His life for the human race, was based on the unchangeable promise of God. Therefore, Christ is regarded as "the Lamb slain from the foundation of the world." So this divine agreement, which was reached before the world began, was confirmed at Calvary when Jesus ratified it with His own blood. "Before the foundations of the earth were laid, the Father and the Son had united in a covenant to redeem man if he should be overcome by Satan. They had clasped Their hands in a solemn pledge that Christ should become the surety for the human race. This pledge Christ has fulfilled" (*The Desire of Ages*, p. 834).

Several Messianic implications in chapters 12 and 13 relate to Christ's sacrifice: (1) the pierced Messiah (12:10), (2) the fountain opened for cleansing (13:1), (3) the wounds in His hands (13:6), (4) and the sword of God against His Shepherd and Fellow (13:7).

The Piercing. Just before Christ was pierced on the cross, Judas betrayed Him for 30 shekels, the price of a common slave. The Jewish leaders' eagerness to get rid of Christ reveals their total contempt and ingratitude. The all-worthy Christ was treated as worthless by His own ungrateful people, yet He treated the unworthy as worth everything. Even in His anguish on the cross, He looked at His tormentors and uttered these moving words, "Father, forgive them; for they know not what they do" (Luke 23:34).

In connection with this "piercing," Zechariah 12:10 introduces a new element of mourning and supplication that God will pour out on the inhabitants of Jerusalem. Apparently a prominent servant of God had been martyred through the intrigue and spiritual blindness of the leaders. Then mourning and remorse gripped them after they fully realized what they had done.

The "piercing" of verse 10 has more than one application. Zechariah in this context is envisioning what the Jews might have done if they had prepared themselves and others for the first advent of Christ. Certainly Jesus would have died, but not at their hands. And they would have mourned Him greatly in the spirit of repentance and gratitude, realizing that He generously sacrificed Himself for their sins and the sins of the world. (See *The SDA Bible Commentary*, vol. 4, p. 1113.)

Tragically, Israel as a nation rejected the gift of God's beloved Son. "Jerusalem had been the child of His care, and as a tender father mourns over a wayward son, so Jesus wept over the beloved city. How can I give thee up? . . . One soul is of such value that, in comparison with it, worlds sink into insignificance; but here was a whole nation to be lost. When the fast westering sun should pass . . . , Jerusalem's day of grace would be ended" (*The Desire of Ages*, pp. 577, 578).

We may find another limited application right after

Pentecost, when Peter presented this "pierced" Messiah to the Jews as the one they had crucified (Acts 2:23). Then in verse 37 we learn that "when they heard this they were cut to the heart, and said to Peter and the rest of the apostles, 'Brethren, what shall we do?' " That day 3,000 souls, mourning for Christ, were converted and joined the early church.

Furthermore, this Messianic prophecy of grieving for the pierced Jesus will meet a larger fulfillment at His glorious second coming. It is evident from the language John uses in Revelation 1:7, associating the "piercing" of the Messiah with the "mourning" over Him, that he has in mind the context of Zechariah 12:10. Therefore, this regret and mourning for the pierced Messiah will be experienced at the Second Advent by those who despised and pierced Christ during His crucifixion. John also quotes directly Zechariah 12:10 in John 19:37 when he described the piercing of Christ. (See also Matt. 24:30.) "All who have died in the faith of the third angel's message come forth from the tomb glorified. . . . 'They also which pierced Him' (Rev. 1:7), those that mocked and derided Christ's dying agonies, and the most violent opposers of His truth and His people, are raised to behold Him in His glory" (*The Great Controversy*, p. 637).

"The very men who thrust the spear into the side of the Lord of life will behold the print of the spear and will lament with deep anguish the part which they acted in marring His body" (*Early Writings*, p. 179).

The Fountain. The phrase "on that day" there shall be a fountain opened for cleansing (Zech. 13:1) hearkens back to "in one day" (Zech. 3:9, KJV), when the iniquity of the land would be removed. It is the same day also when Jesus was pierced (Zech. 12:10). In a sense, there had always been a fountain open for forgiveness and cleansing in the Lamb slain before the world. Before the cross, by faith people looked to that fountain—something we must always do even after the cross. The force of the Hebrew words indicates that the fountain not only shall be opened, but shall remain open. This continual flow has been available freely and efficaciously to all humanity throughout history.

The background of this figurative term, "a fountain opened," is rooted in the Levitical ritual. The water of expiation was used to purify and consecrate the Levites (Num. 8:7). Also Ezekiel mentions the purifying effect of sprinkling water on the children of Israel. "I will sprinkle clean water upon you, and you shall be clean from all your uncleannesses" (Eze. 36:25). However, in Zechariah 13:1 there is no sprinkling, but complete washing from the opened fountain. A fountain suggests an abundant and ever-flowing supply for the cleansing of sin. It is more than sufficient to clean the most defiled. It is not a cleansing from ceremonial defilement, but the purification from spiritual defilement of the inward being. "That flowing stream was a symbol of the ever-flowing, ever-cleansing efficacy of the blood of Christ . . . the fountain that was open for Judah and Jerusalem, wherein they may wash and be clean from every stain of sin. We are to have free access to the atoning blood of Christ" (*The SDA Bible Commentary*, Ellen G. White Comments, vol. 1, p. 1111).

The Jewish leaders were so particular in "keeping" the Sabbath that they asked Pilate to send his soldiers so that they might break the legs of the crucified men, including Jesus. That way they could be sure that the victims would die so they could take their bodies away before the Sabbath began. Ironically, the Jewish leaders were "keeping" the Sabbath while murdering the Lord of the Sabbath and wanting to break His bones! John tells us that when the soldiers came to Jesus, they found Him already dead, so there was no need to break His legs. Surprised that Jesus had died so quickly, one soldier, to be doubly certain, pierced His side with a spear. At once a stream of blood and water gushed forth (John 19:31-37; see also Ps. 34:20). "The priests and rulers were amazed to find that Christ was dead. Death by the cross was a lingering process; it was difficult to determine when life had ceased. It was an unheard-of thing for one to die within six hours of crucifixion. The priests wished to make sure of the death of Jesus, and at their suggestion a soldier thrust a spear into the Saviour's side"

(*The Desire of Ages*, pp. 771, 772).

But why did our Saviour die much sooner than expected? Was it because of His tremendous physical suffering? No. "It was not the spear thrust, it was not the pain of the cross, that caused the death of Jesus. That cry, uttered 'with a loud voice,' at the moment of death, the stream of blood and water that flowed from His side, declared that He died of a *broken heart*. His heart was broken by mental anguish. He was slain by the sin of the world" (*ibid.*, p. 772; italics supplied).

That precious stream of blood and water mentioned in John 19:34 seems to merge the "piercing" of Zechariah 12:10 with the "fountain opened" in Zechariah 13:1. In commenting on this stream, Ellen White writes, "There came out two distinct streams, one of blood, the other of water. The blood was to wash away the sins of those who should believe in His name, and the water was to represent that living water which is obtained from Jesus to give life to the believer" (*Early Writings*, p. 209).

The Wounds in His Hands. Zechariah 12:10, 13:1, and 13:6, 7 have something significant in common. They show three interrelated events relating to Christ's suffering and death. These important events are respectively (1) the piercing of Christ, (2) the opening of the fountain for cleansing, and (3) the wounded hands of the smitten Good Shepherd. There is no doubt that the first two verses above refer to the same person, namely the Messiah, but who is Zechariah 13:6 alluding to?

Bible students raise the question as to the identity of this person. There seems to be some ambiguity regarding who this individual was who was asked, "What are these wounds in your hands?" Careful study of the four verses that precede this question has indicated to a number of students that the context deals with an act of sanctification introduced and made possible by the fountain opened for cleansing from sin (verse 1). The two specific sins alluded to are idolatry and false prophecy, which were widespread at that time.

At first glance the context of verses 2-6 seems to point to a supposedly converted false prophet who got wounded in connection with idolatrous worship and who was trying to conceal that fact by dismissing his wounds as resulting from a squabble with his friends. But when I consider carefully the context of the piercing of Christ in Zechariah 12:10, the fountain opened in Zechariah 13:1, and the smitten Shepherd in verse 7, I conclude that consistency leads me to deduce that the person with wounds in his hands is the suffering Messiah. Also verse 6 seems to go together with verse 7, for it commences a new thought about the wounds and leads logically to and reinforces verse 7 about the smitten Shepherd. So the one pierced in the side, the one wounded in the hands, and the one smitten by God is the Christ who in His person became a fountain opened for cleansing and redemption.

The SDA Bible Commentary explains that "some interpreters have applied this text to Christ as predictive of His scourging and wounds received at the hands of those who should have been His friends. . . . This must be done by secondary application or by making a break after Zechariah 13:5 and by connecting verse 6 with verse 7, which is clearly predictive of Christ (Matt. 26:31)" (vol. 4, p. 1115).

It is clear, however, from *The Acts of the Apostles*, page 226, that Ellen White understood Zechariah 13:6 to refer to Christ. She writes, "Even the manner of His death had been shadowed forth. . . . 'One shall say unto him, What are these wounds in thine hands? Then He shall answer, Those with which I was wounded in the house of my friends.' "

It is astounding that Christ calls these whose hands were stained with His blood, "My friends!" This innocent blood of Christ does not cry out in vengeance over those who spilled it. His blood flows as a continuous stream of forgiveness and love. The wounded hands are not clenched defiantly, but are stretched forth to embrace us in reconciliation. We ourselves deserved to be pierced, wounded, and smitten, but He took the initiative to die in our place. We did not have to appease Him with our wounds as the heathen do for their gods, for "he was wounded for our transgressions, he was bruised for our iniquities" (Isa. 53:5).

The Sword of God Against His Shepherd. Like a captain of an army stands ready to unsheath his mighty sword to exact retribution against his enemies, so also does God the Lord of hosts unsheath His sword of divine justice against our Substitute. God declares in Zechariah 13:7, "Awake, O sword, against My Shepherd, against the Man who is My Companion" (NKJV). What implications may we glean relating to the nature of the Shepherd from the use of the terms *man* and *companion*?

The Shepherd Messiah is fully divine and fully human, the perfect mediator between God and man. Yes, the Shepherd is a "Man," but He is also God's "Companion." The word *companion* in Hebrew refers to fellowship, friendship, and closeness in communion and vocation. He is the closest to the Father, for They are one (John 10:30). He is Man, the Word made flesh (John 1:14), but He is also the mighty God and the everlasting Father (Isa. 9:6).

Jesus applied this prophecy to Himself (Matt. 26:31) when He was ready to offer Himself on the cross and the disciples were to be scattered. (See also Matt. 26:56; John 16:32; Isa. 53:10.)

"Of the suffering Saviour Jehovah Himself declared through Zechariah, 'Awake, O sword, against my shepherd, and against the man that is my fellow.' Zechariah 13:7. As the substitute and surety for sinful man, Christ was to suffer under divine justice. . . . He was to know what it means for sinners to stand before God without an intercessor" (*Prophets and Kings*, p. 691). Also, after quoting 13:7, Ellen White writes, "Hitherto He had been an intercessor for others; now He longed to have an intercessor for Himself" (*The Desire of Ages*, p. 686).

Christ
the Victorious King

"And the Lord will become king over all the earth; on that day the Lord will be one and his name one" (Zech. 14:9). On that day there will be no more powers or principalities, human or demonic; there will be no other gods, allegiances, or conflicts, because Christ the triumphant king will conclude the great controversy, eradicate all evil, and establish Himself as the supreme and sovereign ruler over the whole earth. Soon the prophetic Stone, whirling with divine force, will smite all human and satanic kingdoms, shattering them to pieces. He will Himself become a great mountain and fill the whole earth (Dan. 2:34, 35).

Throughout the prophecies of Zechariah the Messiah repeatedly strove to restore His people prior to and following His first advent. But now in chapter 14 we catch a glimpse of Christ's third coming, which comes immediately at the end of the millennium. Here in the final chapter of Zechariah we see God's final and ultimate act of restoration. Thank God for the first and the second advents of Christ, but what would be the final outcome of the great controversy without the third advent? There would not be ultimate restoration.

In this wicked world, we are so accustomed to seeing suffering, evil, and death that sometimes it seems impossible for us to imagine that all this will finally end. But end they will! Christ at His third coming will bring complete and final restoration. What a day that will be! No more suffering or sickness, no more sin and death, and no more Satan, for the former things will all pass away, and Christ will make all things new (Rev. 21:2-5).

It would be useful at the outset to clarify some points relevant to the apocalyptic/eschatological predictions alluded to in our study. We must keep in mind that a tangle of interpretations exist today regarding Zechariah's prophecies, particularly chapter 14. Some guidelines gleaned from *The SDA Bible Commentary* may help us in our task:

1. The promises and prophecies originally applied to literal Israel. They would be fulfilled on condition of their obedience and loyalty to God (vol. 4, p. 25).

2. Many of these promises and prophecies will be realized in spiritual Israel, the church, in the last days (*ibid.*, p. 26).

3. We must take into consideration the New Testament applications of such Old Testament promises and predictions (*ibid.*, p. 38).

4. Prophecies sometimes have a dual application—fulfillment during the prophet's time as well as in the future (*ibid.*, p. 37).

5. The Old Testament prophecies that will be fulfilled through the church will be fulfilled in principle but not necessarily in every detail and particularity (*ibid.*, p. 37).

One question that many wonder and speculate about regarding the interpretation of Zechariah's predictions has to do with the establishment of the modern state of Israel. The apostle Paul affirms that God's rejection of literal Israel and its mission to evangelize the world does not mean the rejection of individual Jews. All peoples of the world have an equal opportunity to accept the gospel and join spiritual Israel (the Christian church) be they Jews or otherwise. (See Rom. 9-11.) A real spiritual Israelite is one who is converted in his heart to Christ no matter what race or color he may represent. And all members of spiritual Israel are one in Christ, forming the spiritual seed of Abraham (Gal. 3:9, 28, 29).

"But when the Jews rejected Christ there was no such assurance of reinstatement. The present-day return of the

Jews to Palestine and the establishment of the modern state of Israel do not imply reinstatement as God's people, present or future. Whatever the Jews, as a nation, may do, now or in time to come, is in no way related to the former promises made to them. . . . Any idea that the return of the Jews to their ancestral home, that is, to the new state of Israel, may in any way be related to Bible prophecy is without valid scriptural foundation. It ignores the plain statements of the Old Testament that God's promises to Israel were all conditional" (*The SDA Bible Commentary*, vol. 4, p. 33).

On That Day. This expression is often used in the Bible to describe the time when God intervenes in the affairs of this world in order to punish the wicked, to chastise or deliver His people, and, at the end of the world, to vanquish all the world kingdoms, deliver His faithful remnant, and establish His own everlasting kingdom.

Even though the expression "on that day" is used throughout Zechariah, it becomes dominant in the closing chapters, particularly chapter 14. It appears only two times in chapters 1-8; however, it appears 19 times in chapters 9-14 and as many as 14 times in chapters 12-14. It is mentioned eight times in chapter 14 alone. Clearly, the apocalyptic and eschatological spirit becomes progressively dominant and more intensified toward the end of the book. Chapter 14 deals with this theme, as do the other chapters mentioned, but with increasing intensity as it gathers momentum toward the events in the last days when God will put a complete and final end to evil.

Jerusalem's Only Defense. The real strength of God's people never comes through human power but "through the Lord of hosts, their God" (Zech. 12:5). The real strength of Israel was always found in their trust and confidence in God and in their obedience to His will. He always wanted to fight in their behalf, for the battle is His to win (Zech. 14:3). And in connection with "on that day" we notice some specific and interesting imageries employed in chapters 12 and 13 to illustrate how God is His people's strength. We will look at a couple of them in chapter 12.

God will make Jerusalem a cup of reeling to her enemies (verse 2). Imagine different powers gathering around to drink from a big cup. They desire to finish off Jerusalem, swallowing it like wine in a cup. But in drinking the wine, they become powerless and flounder as drunkards. The cup remains standing because it is established in the Lord.

Another interesting imagery is the heavy stone into which God will make Jerusalem (verse 3). He will make His people a sharp-edged boulder that is half embedded in the ground. This farming imagery depicts stones that the farmers could not uproot from the land. Those who try to get rid of it shall end up themselves bruised. So in trying to hurt Jerusalem, they only hurt themselves, and the heavy stone remains firm because it is anchored in the Lord.

The Remnant Tested and Refined. Zechariah 13:9 mentions fire as a means of testing and refining that the remnant must go through. The term *remnant* in itself refers to those who survive severe trials and hardships. God will "refine them as one refines silver, and test them as gold is tested" (Zech. 13:9). The last remnant will and must pass through the fiery furnace to be refined. This experience is an integral part of being a follower of Christ (2 Tim. 3:12). Peter admonishes us that trials test the genuineness of our faith (1 Peter 1:6, 7).

Ellen White associates the testing and refining of the remnant with the time of trouble just before Christ returns. She vividly addresses our spiritual needs and condition as we await His second coming. She explains that the remnant needs to go through the fiery furnace because "their earthliness must be consumed." Then she continues, "The season of distress and anguish before us will require a faith that can endure weariness, delay, and hunger—a faith that will not faint though severely tried. . . . The 'time of trouble, such as never was,' is soon to open upon us; and we shall need an experience which we do not now possess and which many are too indolent to obtain" (*The Great Controversy*, pp. 621, 622).

As we move from the end of chapter 13 to 14:2, we notice a sudden shift from the Lord and the nations that attack Jerusalem (Zech. 14:2) to the Lord's intervention in behalf of Jerusalem against those nations (verse 3). We seem to see here apocalyptic tensions between a rebellious Jerusalem, on the one hand, and a faithful remnant in its midst, on the other hand. This remnant within the remnant likely results from the fiery trials of testing mentioned in Zechariah 13:9.

This may have some ramifications for the "time of shaking" in these last days, when a pure remnant of the remnant will overcome through Christ. We may conclude that judgment will proceed from the people of God (to shake away the unfaithful remnant and to refine the faithful ones) on to the nations. During that time, even some people from these nations will join God's faithful remnant of the remnant to replace the unfaithful ones shaken away, thus constituting a final and universal remnant prepared to meet God. "Standard after standard was left to trail in the dust as company after company from the Lord's army joined the foe and tribe after tribe from the ranks of the enemy united with the commandment-keeping people of God" (*Testimonies*, vol. 8, p. 41).

On the Mount of Olives. Biblically and spiritually the Mount of Olives is significant—especially because it is associated with the life and ministry of Christ in the New Testament. The Mount of Olives rises only 200 feet higher than the Jerusalem Temple area, from which it is separated by the Kidron Valley. Even at this height, it is one of the highest hills in Palestine. The name appears only twice in the Old Testament—once in 2 Samuel 15:30 and again in Zechariah 14:4—the text under consideration. However, the name appears 12 times in the New Testament, especially in connection with Christ. He frequently spent the night there. He entered Jerusalem from it as a humble king riding on an ass. He gave the sermon on His coming and the end of the world from it. His final suffering occurred in the Garden of Gethsemane, located on its slopes. His ascension to heaven took place from it, and there the angels promised the disciples that He would return in the same manner.

In commenting on Christ's feet standing on the Mount of Olives on that day, *The SDA Bible Commentary* explains that some of the details of this prediction will be fulfilled when Christ comes from heaven at the end of the millennium. "The detailed picture is in terms of how these events would have worked out if Jerusalem had stood forever" (vol. 4, p. 1117).

Zechariah continues his prediction of this great event by declaring that "the Lord your God will come, and all the holy ones with him" (Zech. 14:5). The Revised Standard Version gives the literal translation of the Hebrew term *qedoshim*—"holy ones"—which refers to both the redeemed and the angels. In the Old Testament the same word applies also to both. (See Deut. 33:2, 3; Ps. 30:4.) Therefore, at the end of the millennium, Christ the King, accompanied by His angels and the redeemed of all ages whom He took to heaven at His second advent, will descend on the Mount of Olives.

As Christ, escorted by His holy ones, descends upon the Mount of Olives, it will not bear up under His feet. It will split in the middle—east and west—forming a great valley (Zech. 14:4, 5. See Hab. 3:6; Micah 1:3, 4). We can observe several features in common between Revelation 20-22 and Zechariah 14 that should help us to understand more clearly some of the details applicable to Christ's postmillennial advent. But we need to remember that sometimes John mentions the broad view of these events, and then he regresses to describe their specific details.

Studying carefully Zechariah 14, Revelation 20-22, and Ellen White's comments, we glean this chronology of events in connection with the third advent: 1. Christ descends with His holy ones on the Mount of Olives, preparing it to receive the Holy City; and as He descends He resurrects the wicked of all ages. 2. The Holy City descends and rests where Jesus and His holy ones stand. 3. Christ and the holy ones enter the Holy City. 4. The resurrected wicked, led by Satan and his evil hosts, march against and surround the Holy City.

This is "Gog and Magog" or an aspect of the battle of Armageddon. 5. Christ appears on a great white throne to execute judgment against Satan and all his evil hosts. 6. Fire comes down from heaven, consuming them and cleansing the earth. 7. Christ creates a new heaven and a new earth to be the eternal abode of the redeemed. The great controversy finally comes to an end.

"At the close of the thousand years, Christ again returns to the earth. He is accompanied by the host of the redeemed and attended by a retinue of angels. As He descends in terrific majesty He bids the wicked dead arise. . . . Christ descends upon the Mount of Olives, whence, after His resurrection, He ascended." Then Ellen White immediately quotes Zechariah 14:5, 4, 9 and continues, "As the New Jerusalem . . . comes down out of heaven, it rests upon the place purified and made ready to receive it, and Christ, with His people and angels, enters the Holy City" (*The Great Controversy*, pp. 662, 663).

In *Early Writings* we find several pertinent statements relating to Christ's third advent, which the reader is encouraged to study. Here it will suffice to quote just one such important statement. "With Jesus at our head we all descended from the city down to this earth, on a great and mighty mountain, which could not bear Jesus up, and it parted asunder, and there was a mighty plain. Then we looked up and saw the great city. . . . And it came and settled on the place where we stood" (pp. 17, 18; see also pp. 51, 52, 291).

Internal evidence in Zechariah 14 seems to indicate that Christ's descent on the Mount of Olives will be His third coming, which takes place at the conclusion of the millennium and which finds correlation with passages drawn from Revelation 21, 22: 1. Jesus comes with the "holy ones," including the redeemed who were caught up in the clouds to meet Him in the air at His second coming (1 Thess. 4:16, 17) a thousand years earlier (Zech. 14:4, 5; Rev. 20:4, 5). 2. There will be continuous day or light in the earth made new, but during the millennium the earth will be desolate (Zech.

14:6,7; Rev. 21:23; 22:5). 3. "Living waters shall flow out from Jerusalem" (Zech. 14:8), the eternal home of the redeemed (see also Rev. 22:1). 4. Jerusalem will dwell in perfect security. There will be no more curse, and everything will be holy (Zech. 14:11, 21; Rev. 21:27). 5. The Lord will become the king over all the earth cleansed from all evil (Zech. 14:9; Rev. 21:1-4).

The Final Judgment and the New Earth. Satan is set loose for a brief time to deceive the nations. His eyes scan the billions of his followers throughout the ages—by far the greatest army ever—and he attempts for the final time what he has been attempting since his fall, to dethrone God and take His place. It is also an act of desperation and hopelessness on his part, for he knows well that time is short and that this is his last chance. So he and his evil angels lead this universal and gigantic army, assuring them that there is a fighting chance to overtake the small remnant of God and the Holy City. Who knows, Satan might reason, maybe when Christ sees so many billions of His creatures whom He died for He might possibly change His plan.

They all march toward the Holy City. They wait for Satan, their commander in chief, to give his order to launch the attack. Immediately Christ preempts Satan and appears in all His majesty on the great white throne above the city, where He pronounces and executes the final judgment (Rev. 20:11-15). Then "fire came down from heaven and consumed them" (verse 9; see also Rev. 20:7, 8, 10, 14, 15; Eze. 28:6-8; Mal. 4:1; 2 Peter 3:10). Zechariah in graphic and fitting language describes how the Lord will defend Jerusalem against its enemies. He will make Jerusalem "like a blazing pot in the midst of wood, like a flaming torch among sheaves" (Zech. 12:6). He also "will smite all the peoples that wage war against Jerusalem: their flesh shall rot while they are still on their feet, their eyes shall rot in their sockets, and their tongues shall rot in their mouths" (Zech. 14:12).

Finally, at last sin and death will be eradicated. Satan and his followers will never rise again (Nahum 1:9). The earth is purified with a flood of fire. No residue of evil will appear anywhere. And Christ will create a glorious new heaven and new earth, for "no eye has seen, nor ear heard, nor the heart of man conceived, what God has prepared for those who love him" (1 Cor. 2:9). But by far the greatest experience will be to live with our Redeemer forever, for where Jesus is there will be perfect love, peace, and joy. His great desire and ours will be fulfilled in Jesus' promise, "that where I am you may be also" (John 14:3).

In the days of Noah, God provided His faithful remnant with the ark to preserve them from the flood of water. When God destroys and cleanses the earth, He will also provide the ark of the Holy City, New Jerusalem.

We are privileged to learn from Scripture how God has dealt with His people for thousands of years. May we learn valuable lessons from their experience, and be prepared to meet our Lord when He comes. May we prepare ourselves and others to enter that city, whose builder and maker is God.

"The great controversy is ended. Sin and sinners are no more. The entire universe is clean. One pulse of harmony and gladness beats through the vast creation. From Him who created all, flow life and light and gladness, throughout the realms of illimitable space. From the minutest atom to the greatest world, all things, animate and inanimate, in their unshadowed beauty and perfect joy, declare that God is love" (*The Great Controversy*, p. 678).